new steps in
religious education

BOOK 1

THIRD EDITION

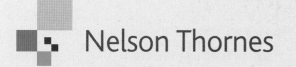

Nelson Thornes

Michael Keene

First edition published in 1991.
Second edition published in 1997.
Third edition published in 2002 by:
Nelson Thornes Ltd
Delta Place
27 Bath Road
CHELTENHAM
GL53 7TH
United Kingdom

11 / 10 9

A catalogue record for this book is available from the British Library

First edition ISBN 0-871402-37-9
Second edition ISBN 0-7487-3079-6
Third edition ISBN10 0-7487-6454-2
          ISBN13 978-0-7487-6454-9

Illustrations by Richard Morris and Julie Nash
Edited by Melanie Gray
Page make-up by Clare Park

Printed and bound in China by 1010 Printing International Ltd

Acknowledgements

The author and publishers wish to thank the following for permission to reproduce photographs and other copyright material in this book:

Corbis p 107; Trip p 106, Trip/B Dhanjal p 104; Trip/H Rogers p 128; All other photographs supplied by The Walking Camera.

Every effort has been made to contact copyright holders and the publishers apologise to anyone whose rights have been inadvertently overlooked and will be happy to rectify any errors or omissions.

The scripture quotations (except where specifically indicated in the text) are taken from the Holy Bible, New International Version®. Copyright © 1973, 1978, 1984 by International Bible Society. Used by permission of International Bible Society. 'NIV' and 'New International Version' are trademarks registered in the United States Patent and Trademark office by International Bible Society.

Throughout the series the terms BCE (Before Common Era) and CE (Common Era) are used instead of the more familiar BC and AD. However, in practice, they mean the same thing.

Contents

Introducing religion

Introduction

Seven out of every ten people in Britain describe themselves as being 'religious'. For most people this seems to mean that they believe in someone or something greater than themselves. They usually call this greater power 'God'. Worshipping God is the most important religious activity, and prayer or meditation is a very important part of that worship. Many people feel it is their duty to worship God.

The two sides of religion

There are two sides to every religion:

- The private side. Although many religious people spend time meeting with other worshippers, it is usually the private side of their religious experience which has the greater impact. Many Christians find time each day to read the **Bible** and pray on their own. In the Jewish faith, the most important religious activities are those that take place at home and not in a **synagogue**. In a Hindu home, each day starts with prayers and offerings made in front of the home **shrine**. This helps people to focus their mind on God before the day begins. Even when people are praying with others, as in a **mosque**, everyone is praying individually to **Allah**.

- The public side. Most religious people do not feel happy only worshipping and praying to God on their own. They need the help and support of others who think and feel as they do about God. This is why most Christians go to a **church**, Jews attend their local synagogue, Muslim men go to a mosque each week for Friday prayers, Sikhs meet together in a **gurdwara**, Hindus gather in a **mandir** and Buddhists meet for meditation in a **temple**. **Muhammad** told his followers that prayers offered together are 25 times more effective than those offered privately.

In this unit

In this unit you will read about the following:

- We will be looking at the six religions which can truly claim to be worldwide faiths – Christianity, Judaism, Islam, Hinduism, Sikhism and Buddhism. Although each of these religions has a special character of its own, they also have much in common.

- All these religions, except Buddhism, believe in God. Buddhism sets out a way of understanding and overcoming the problem of suffering. The other faiths, however, stress the importance of worshipping God as a spiritual activity. By worshipping regularly each follower is able to show what they really think and believe about God. For many people worshipping God is at the very heart of their religious faith.

- All religions teach that there must be a close link between what people believe and how they live. When someone follows a particular religion, he or she expects their faith to affect how they dress and what they eat.

- All religions emphasise the importance of prayer in the spiritual life, although Buddhism speaks of meditation rather than prayer. Prayer is the way in which people communicate with God.

In the glossary

Allah	Mosque
Bible	Muhammad
Church	Shrine
Gurdwara	Synagogue
Mandir	Temple

Looking for God

For many people, religion helps them to answer some very important questions, such as:

- Is there a God?
- How can I know God?
- What is God like?
- What does God ask of me?

It is difficult to be certain about the answers to these questions. In all religious answers, there is a large amount of faith involved. Faith means trusting in those things you cannot understand. Whether or not God exists is largely a matter of faith. Some arguments have been put forward, however, to persuade people to believe in God. This is because people have been looking for God for centuries.

Looking for God

For many years people have put forward arguments to try to convince others that God exists. Here are four arguments:

1 *The cosmological argument.* This argument states that the universe exists, this planet exists and human beings exist. We can be certain about this. None of them, however, could have brought themselves into existence. All require something, or someone, greater than them to have done this. Christianity, Judaism, Islam and Sikhism all teach that the creator of everything that exists is God.

2 *The 'design' argument.* Towards the end of the eighteenth century, the writer and philosopher William Paley asked his readers to imagine walking down a street and finding a watch at their feet. If you opened up the back of the watch, you would see a very complicated piece of machinery working perfectly. Did the watch come into existence after an explosion at a watch factory, or was it made by a highly skilled watchmaker? Surely a watchmaker was involved. The world itself is much more complicated than a watch. Who could have made it but God?

3 *The religious experience argument.* Nearly all religious people claim to have 'experienced' God. Perhaps they have seen a miracle or had an answer to their prayers. They may have become 'religious' after spending many years as a non-believer. Whatever the reason,

A Many people look to God for the answers to some important questions

B Faith is involved in all religions

most religious people believe that they have 'come to know' God in some way. Therefore, because someone has 'experienced' God, God must exist.

4 *The moral argument.* Some people wonder whether we would know the difference between right and wrong unless God had told us. Most of us, for example, know it is wrong to kill, steal and lie. We know this because God has 'revealed' the truth to us. This revelation is written down and recorded in the holy books, such as the Bible, the **Qur'an**, the **Torah** and the **Guru Granth Sahib**.

Many people who are searching for God look to the main religions. Others do not find answers to their questions there and so look elsewhere. There are others who have concluded that there is no point in looking for God since He does not exist.

In the glossary
Guru Granth Sahib   **Torah**
Qur'an

 Find the answers

- Who, according to many religions, is the creator of everything?

- Who said that our complicated universe must have been designed?

- What are the names of four holy books?

Learning about, learning from

1 **a.** Write a short story in which someone thinks they have 'experienced' God in some way.
  b. Do you think human beings can really 'experience' God? Give two reasons for your answer.

2 Write down five 'big' questions you would want any religion to be able to answer. A 'big' question is one that deals with the meaning of life and death.

3 Design a poster to illustrate one of the arguments for the existence of God.

Extra activity

Read the four arguments which have been put forward in support of the existence of God. Think about them carefully. Does any one of them strike you as more convincing than the others? Explain your answer.

God

Words can be used to describe those things that we can see and touch, such as a car or the inside of a building. However, words are often stretched to their limits when we talk about our deepest feelings, such as love or the loss of a loved one. Religious people often say that God is beyond the reach of all human language. Religious worship, and the need to speak to God in prayer, means that some attempt to use words has to be made.

Describing God

People have always known how difficult it is to talk about God. Many have tried in the past to overcome this problem by using opposites to describe what they think He is like – and not like. They have spoken of God as being close to them and yet 'out there', beyond everything. God takes an interest in their lives, helping them with their problems and yet being distant and far away. God is all-powerful and yet sometimes He seems to be unable to help those who pray to Him.

A Hindus believe that images of different gods help them to direct their thoughts and worship to the one true God

Each religion has developed its own words for talking about God. To Muslims, God is called Allah; in Sikhism He is **Nam**; in Hinduism God is **Brahman** and many Christians think of God as their Heavenly Father. Some Jews believe that the name of God is too holy to speak or write. Buddhism, however, is different. The **Buddha** was not concerned with questions about how the world was created or what God was like. He wanted to know what caused suffering and how it could be overcome. Buddhism is a very different religion from the others described in this book.

Images and statues

Christians, Jews, Muslims and Sikhs all believe there is only one God and that it is wrong to make a statue or image of Him in any form. Hinduism, however, teaches that although there is only one God, He can take many forms. There are said to be 330 million different gods and goddesses in Hinduism, and most of them have taken the form of a statue or image at some time or other (picture A). Hindus find these statues help them to understand and worship the one God. Each statue or image of God illustrates a side of the character and personality of Brahman. They can show Him as being male or female, the creator or the destroyer, kind or ruthless. Just as there are so many different sides to the personality of God, so there are many statues. Sometimes a Hindu place of worship (a mandir) is dedicated to one god or goddess and sometimes to many of them. These gods help worshippers to see that the one God is beyond all things and yet has made Himself known to his worshippers.

B The presence of the Sikh holy book – the Guru Granth Sahib – in the gurdwara assures all Sikhs that the True Guru, God, is with them

A modern Hindu story

The Master (a spiritual leader) became a legend in his lifetime. God once sought his advice. 'I want to play a game of hide-and-seek with humankind. I've asked my angels where the best place is to hide. Some say the depths of the ocean. Others the top of the highest mountain. Others still the far side of the moon or a distant star. What do you suggest?' Said the Master: 'Hide in the human heart. That's the last place they will think of.'

In the glossary

Brahman   Nam
Buddha

Find the answers

- What is the Muslim name for God?
- What is the name given to God in Hinduism?
- Which religion does not believe in God?

Learning about, learning from

1 a. List the religions which believe there is one God.
b. Which religion allows statues and images to represent the one God?
c. Why do you think many religions teach that it is wrong to make a statue or image of God?

2 a. Write down five things that many people believe about God.
b. How do you think they created the picture of God in their minds?
c. Throughout their lives, do you think many people change the way they think about God? Do you expect to change your ideas about Him?
d. What ideas do you hold about God at the moment? Explain your answer.

Extra activity

Read the modern Hindu story in the box. It is trying to make a serious point. What do you think that point is?

Beliefs

People ask many questions about life and death. You may ask yourself these questions at some time or other:

- Who am I?
- Where did I come from?
- Why am I on earth?
- Do I matter?
- Why do some people suffer more than others?
- What happens to me after I die?
- Where did the world come from?

Faith

For some people, religion provides the answers to these questions. Of course, no one can prove that any of the answers are the right ones. These answers are called 'beliefs' and this is just what they are. The way in which people trust the answers and

A The most important Christian belief is that **Jesus** was crucified and that, three days later, he rose from the dead

use them to give meaning to their own lives is called 'faith'. Some people believe in their faith strongly and look to it for all the answers. Others belong to a religion but sometimes doubt the answers it gives.

Each religion has its own set of beliefs. The Christian belief in God, for example, is very different from the Muslim belief in Allah, although followers of both religions believe in an all-powerful God who made the world. There are similarities between the various religions but there are important differences too.

Even within the same religion people do not necessarily believe the same thing. The **Anglican Church** and **Roman Catholic Church**, for example, both belong to the Christian Church. They share many beliefs but disagree over others. This is the reason why there are many different Christian Churches and not just one.

Belief and atheism

Although ways of worshipping in a religion may change over time, beliefs remain largely the same. This is because followers think these beliefs were 'revealed' by God. These revelations were recorded in such holy books as the Bible, the Qur'an and the Guru Granth Sahib. The religions teach that these revelations do not change. If the revelations in the holy books do not change, the beliefs based on them do not change either.

As we saw on page 4, seven out of every ten people in Britain describe themselves as being 'religious'. This leaves a large number of people who fit into one of two groups:

- **Agnostics** – those who are not sure whether God exists or not.
- **Atheists** – those who have reached the conclusion that God does not exist.

B In Sikhism, the clothes that a person wears to worship express important beliefs

In the glossary

Agnostics   Jesus
Anglican Church   Roman Catholic
Atheists   Church

Find the answers

• What is the difference between 'belief' and 'faith'?

• What is an agnostic?

• What is an atheist?

Learning about, learning from

1 The Shahadah is the basic belief of all Muslims. It is written in Arabic. Translated into English it says: 'There is no god but Allah and Muhammad is God's messenger.'
   a. What is the Muslim name for God?
   b. Do Muslims believe in one God or many gods?
   c. Name two beliefs held by Muslims.

2 Members of the same religion do not always believe the same things.
   a. Do you and other members of your family agree about everything?
   b. Describe two things you have disagreements about.
   c. Does it matter that you do not always agree?

3 Many people are puzzled about life after death.
   a. Do you find it important to believe in a life after death? Explain your answer.
   b. If there is a life after death, what do you imagine it might be like?
   c. If you believe in a life after death, do you think it makes any difference to the way that you live your life now?

Extra activity

Imagine if the answer to everything could be found on the internet. What would be the first question you would type in? What would make you believe the answer?

Worship

People worshipped God long before they built special buildings for that purpose. The wonders of nature reminded them of the presence of God. For many people they still do today – at least, when the sun is shining!

Holy buildings

As each religion gained more followers, special buildings in which to worship became necessary. Some of these religious buildings are large, as worship can bring together many people. You will discover this for yourself if you visit a **cathedral**, which is a special kind of church. Here, as in other places of worship, you may find people praying, singing, chanting, dancing, listening or simply sitting quietly. Everyone tries to worship God in the way that best suits them.

A religious building is one that is dedicated to the worship of God, whether it be a church (picture A), a synagogue, a mosque, a mandir (picture B), a gurdwara or a Buddhist shrine. Some religious buildings are centuries old, and many generations of people have gathered there to sing hymns, say prayers, offer up praise and listen to the holy scriptures being read. This link between the past and the present is important in all faiths. Some

religious buildings, however, are more modern and have been built on new housing estates or elsewhere because this is where most people now live. New faiths have also arrived in Britain over the last century and followers have built places of worship or adapted other buildings.

Atmosphere

Often the worship that goes on in a religious building can be noisy. In the **Salvation Army**, for example, the singing of hymns is accompanied by a brass band and by the shaking of tambourines. Worship can also be quiet and thoughtful. When **Quakers** come together on a **Sunday** morning, most of their worship time is spent in silent prayer and reflection. Buddhists, too, usually meditate in silence.

Most worshippers say that the atmosphere inside their place of worship is extremely important. Each religion has its own way of creating an atmosphere which encourages worshippers to act 'appropriately' in the presence of God. Some religions, for example, ask that worshippers wash themselves and put on clean clothes before coming to offer worship. Both Islam and Sikhism ask that worshippers remove their shoes as they enter the mosque or gurdwara, to show respect for God. Each act of worship brings God and the worshipper closer together and that cannot happen unless the worshipper behaves in a dignified and respectful way.

A This is a typical parish church, where Christians have worshipped for centuries

---

In the glossary

Cathedral	Salvation Army
Quakers	Sunday

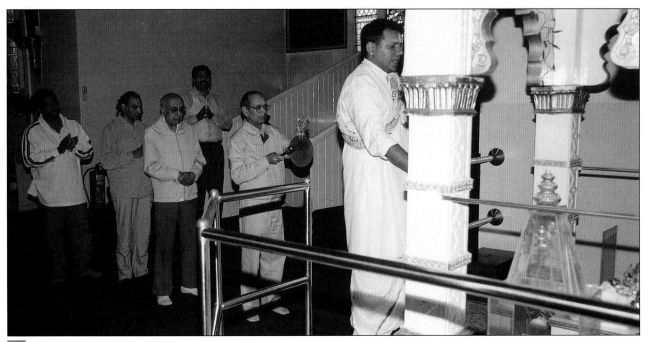

B Although many Hindus meet together in a mandir to worship, others feel happier just worshipping at home

Find the answers

- What are you likely to find going on in a place of worship?

- What is the main difference between Salvation Army and Quaker worship?

- How do some people show respect as they come to worship?

Learning about, learning from

1 The names of six different places of worship are mentioned on these pages. Make a list of them and find out who worships in each.

2 Pictures A and B show people taking part in different acts of worship. Look at the photographs carefully. Discuss each of them with your teacher and other members of your class. Explain in a sentence or two how you might feel if you were taking part in each act of worship.

3 Most religious people say they are expressing their deepest feelings when they worship. If you wanted to express your deepest feelings, how would you do it? Would you dance, sing, be quiet or do something else?

Extra activity

Many people prefer to worship at home than to go to a place of worship. Explain why.

Prayer

For most religious people prayer, or meditation, is the most important thing they do. It is found, in one form or another, in all religions. Prayer is a way of making contact with God. Some people, such as **monks** and **nuns**, devote themselves to a lifetime of prayer, but most people have to find time to fit it into a busy, everyday life.

What is prayer?

In all religions, people who pray are:

- worshipping God by showing their devotion and respect, as well as thanking God for all His goodness to them
- confessing their sins (wrongdoings) to God so that they can be forgiven
- asking for God's help in their everyday lives
- seeking God's blessing on others.

Although most people use words while praying, these words can be unspoken or said aloud. As people enter a church, for example, they often bow their heads and pray silently to God. Meditation, another form of prayer, is a kind of inner silence.

It can include concentration on a repeated word or phrase, called a **mantra**, or a short prayer.

Confession and thanksgiving

When people think about God they sometimes become conscious of their own sins and shortcomings. They feel the need to confess those sins and ask for God's forgiveness. In the Roman Catholic Church this takes the form of **confession**, where a person confesses his or her sins to a **priest**. The priest then gives them **absolution** and the assurance that their sins have been forgiven by God.

Knowing that their sins have been forgiven, worshippers come into God's presence aware that they have much to be thankful for. Thanksgiving is a very important part of prayer. In the Jewish faith, for example, it is said that there is a prayer to cover everything that someone might wish to be thankful for. Many religions have special services and prayers so that worshippers can end each day in a thankful frame of mind.

Remembering others

Some people think prayer could be a selfish activity, with people asking God just for the things they want. It certainly could be selfish if people were concerned only with themselves and their own needs. All religions stress, however, that real praying must also include remembering the needs of others. This is called intercession. Praying for others brings worshippers together and shows that the world is one family in which everyone exists to help others in need.

A For this woman, prayer is a private matter between herself and God

B In some religions, such as Judaism, the clothes worn for prayer are an important way of making it a spiritual experience

Jesus and prayer

Jesus said this about prayer:
And when you pray, do not be like the hypocrites, for they love to stand praying in the synagogues and on the street corners to be seen by men... when you pray, go into your room, close the door and pray to your Father, who is unseen... And when you pray, do not keep on babbling like pagans, for they think they will be heard because of their many words.

In the glossary

Absolution	Monks
Confession	Nuns
Mantra	Priest

Find the answers

- Which people devote themselves to a lifetime of prayer?
- What do people sometimes use to help with meditation?
- What is absolution?

Learning about, learning from

1 Explain in a sentence the meaning of the following words.
  a. Worship.
  b. Thanksgiving.
  c. Confession.
  d. Intercession.

2 Read the quotation from Jesus in the box.
  a. Do you know what a 'hypocrite' is? If not, look it up in a dictionary and write down the definition.
  b. How do hypocrites behave and why do you think they were condemned by Jesus?
  c. How should genuine people pray?

3 Look at pictures A and B. Imagine you are one of the people praying. Write down some of the things you might be saying or thinking as you pray.

4 **a.** When you have done something you are ashamed of, do you want to confess it?
  b. Why is confession important for some religious people?

Extra activity

Religious people believe that 'prayer changes things'. What arguments can you suggest for and against this point of view?

Daily life

For most religious people, their beliefs affect the way they live their everyday lives. They affect, in particular, the clothes that they wear and the food that they eat. Here are some examples.

In the Jewish faith

Judaism has important rules about diet. The Jewish holy books lay down strict guidelines about the food that Jews are and are not allowed to eat. Most Jews live by these rules even though they are now thousands of years old. These rules are called **kashrut**.

The Torah lists the animals, birds and fish that are forbidden to all Jews. The food that Jews can eat is called **kosher** ('fit'). This includes any animal that has cloven hoofs and chews the cud. In practice, this means that a Jew cannot eat pork in any form but any meat from cows and sheep is permitted. It is also important that the animal's blood is totally drained out before any meat is eaten. This means that there are strict rules about the way in which the animals are killed.

In the Muslim faith

The teaching of the Qur'an does not allow Muslims to eat pork meat and fat. They are not allowed to drink alcohol or to take part in gambling. The Qur'an also does not allow a person to lend money to someone else and then to charge them interest on it.

In the Hindu faith

Most Hindus do not eat beef as they look upon the cow as a sacred (holy) animal (picture A). In practice, most Hindus are vegetarians because they believe that to kill of any form of life is like murder and so is strictly forbidden.

In the Sikh faith

Guru Nanak, the founder of Sikhism, taught that as food is unimportant it does not really matter what a person eats. Many Sikhs are vegetarians.

The everyday life of religious Sikhs is governed by the **Five Ks**. These are:

- kesh – long hair
- kangha – a comb which keeps the hair tidy
- kara – a steel bracelet worn around the right wrist
- kachs – shorts worn as an undergarment
- kirpan – a short sword carried on the left hip.

The long hair of an adult male Sikh is wrapped up neatly in a **turban** (picture B). A young boy has a simpler form of head-covering, called a patka, but he wears a turban as soon as he can tie one for himself.

A Hindus treat cows as sacred animals

B For a Sikh, long hair is a sign of devotion to God while the turban, by which the hair is covered, shows that the person belongs to the Sikh religion

In the glossary

Five Ks	Kosher
Guru Nanak	Turban
Kashrut	

Find the answers

- What does 'kashrut' mean?

- What does the Qur'an forbid Muslims to do?

- Which two religions forbid their members from eating pork?

Learning about, learning from

1 Look at picture B.
   a. What form of head-covering is this man wearing?
   b. When did he start wearing it?
   c. Which religion does he belong to?

2 Explain in a sentence the meaning of the following words or phrases.
   a. Kosher.
   b. Vegetarian.
   c. Kesh.
   d. Kangha.
   e. The Five Ks.

3 Guru Nanak taught his followers that food is unimportant, but some other religions disagree. Why do you think these religions place such importance on the diet?

4 Alcohol plays an important part in the social lives of many people in Britain, yet it is banned in Muslim countries. Why do you think the Qur'an takes such a strong line against it?

Extra activity

Most religions try to influence the everyday lives of their followers.
a. Why do religions teach that how a person lives day by day has real spiritual importance?
b. Do you think they are right?

2 Religious founders

Introduction

Hinduism, the oldest faith in the world, did not start with a single founder. Judaism can be traced back to two men – **Abraham** and **Moses**. Buddhism began with the teachings of the Buddha, Christianity on the teachings of Jesus, Islam on those of Muhammad and Sikhism largely on the teachings of Guru Nanak. After the death of these founders, their teachings were taken up and spread throughout the world by devoted followers.

Beginnings

The Jewish nation began with Abraham, who lived in a part of the Middle East called the Fertile Crescent about 4000 years ago. Abraham believed that God had spoken to him. At the time, everyone believed in many gods but Abraham came to believe that there was just one God who had made the heavens, the earth and everything that existed. Centuries later, Moses led the descendants of Abraham – the Jews – out of slavery. He gave them their religious laws, called the Torah, which includes the **Ten Commandments**.

Christianity grew out of Judaism because Jesus and most of his followers were Jews. Jesus received his call from God after he had been baptised. Before long, Christianity broke away from Judaism and became a separate religion. Centuries later, Muhammad also received a series of messages from God and these are recorded in the Muslim holy book, the Qur'an. Muslims believe that, although there have been many **prophets** from God, Muhammad was the last – and greatest – of them. Sikhs, too, trace their beginnings back to the life and teachings of a single man, Guru Nanak. Like the others, he heard the call of God through an extraordinary experience.

Buddhism sprang out of the experiences and meditations of Siddhartha Gotama – the Buddha. He believed that he had reached a real insight into the meaning of life. He did not, however, believe that God had communicated with him. This makes him different from the other religious founders.

In this unit

In this unit you will read about the following:

- God made a special agreement with Abraham, which made him the 'father' of the Jewish nation. This agreement was renewed through his son and grandson, Isaac and Jacob.

- Moses was the leader chosen by God to lead the Jews out of slavery and take them to their new home of Israel. On this journey they received the Torah, including the Ten Commandments, on Mount Sinai.

- Muhammad received several revelations from Allah and these form the foundation of Islam. These revelations are recorded in the Qur'an. Muhammad later led his followers against the city of **Makkah** and conquered it. He set up the true worship of Allah at the **Ka'bah** in the city.

- Guru Nanak was the first, and most important, of ten **Gurus** whose teachings form the foundation of Sikhism. He visited heaven and was sent back to earth by God to preach to the people. He visited the Hindu and Muslim holy places with his message before setting up a farming community. Many of his disciples visited him there.

- Siddhartha Gotama was a prince who saw an old man, a sick man, a dead man and a holy man in quick succession. These sights inspired him to search for the answer to suffering. After he was enlightened the Buddha chose to remain on earth to help others in their search for the truth.

In the glossary

Abraham	Moses
Gurus	Prophets
Ka'bah	Ten Commandments
Makkah	

Gurus

This is how Guru Nanak described the work of a guru, a spiritual teacher:
The guru is the ladder, the dinghy, the raft by means of which one reaches God. The guru is the lake, the ocean, the boat, the sacred place of pilgrimage, the river. Without the guru there can be no love.

Abraham

Although Abraham is an important figure to both Christians and Muslims, his importance to Jews is far greater. It was through him that the Jewish nation began. He was born in the Middle East some time between 2000 BCE and 1800 BCE in the town of Ur, on the edge of the Persian Gulf.

Abraham meets God

Abraham's father, Terah, took his family to live in Haran when Abraham was young. You can follow the route they took on map A. As he grew up in Haran, Abraham came to believe in one God instead of the many gods that everyone around him worshipped. He soon felt that this God was calling him to travel, with his family, to the land of Canaan. God promised Abraham that all of this land would soon belong to him and his descendants for ever. To guarantee this, God entered into a covenant (agreement) with Abraham. Under this agreement, God promised Abraham that:

* Abraham, and those who came after him, would have a special relationship with God. Abraham would start a new nation – the Jewish nation.

* God would make special demands on the Jewish people. He would expect them to have different standards from all others. They would be given special laws to help them to do this.

Abraham uprooted his large family, which included many relations and servants, and took them to Canaan. This is the country that is known as **Israel** today. There was only one problem. Abraham and Sarah, his wife, did not have any children of their own and they were now growing very old. It took a miracle from God for Sarah to become pregnant and for a son, Isaac, to be born. The Jewish nation had begun.

B This banner represents the 12 tribes, named after the 12 sons of Jacob, on which the nation of Israel was based

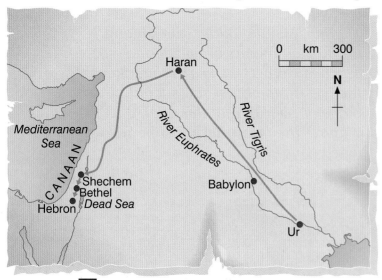

A This map shows the journeys that Abraham's family took from Ur to Haran, and the one that Abraham took in response to the call of God

The Patriarchs

The story of Abraham is told in the most important part of the Jewish scriptures, the Torah. The story goes on to tell us that Abraham was very old when he died. He was succeeded as head of the family by Isaac and then his grandson, Jacob (who later became known as Israel). Jews know Abraham, Isaac and Jacob as the Patriarchs ('father figures') of their faith. The Jewish nation today is seen as being the descendants of Abraham. Jews look back upon Abraham as their father.

Jacob and his descendants spent over 400 years as slaves of the Egyptians, during which time they were treated very harshly. They were put to work building the houses of their Egyptian masters. During this period, however, the number of Jews in Egypt grew steadily. By the time their slavery ended, in the thirteenth century BCE, there were over a million of them. They were led out of Egypt to freedom by Moses. It was Moses who received the Jewish laws, the Torah, from God.

C This window is a reminder that the nation of Israel began with Abraham and the Torah

In the glossary

Israel

Find the answers

- Where and when did Abraham live?
- Why did Abraham travel to Canaan?
- Where in the Jewish scriptures do we find the story of Abraham?

Learning about, learning from

1 **a.** What is a covenant?
  b. There were two sides to the covenant that God made with Abraham. What were they?

2 Read Genesis 22.1–12. Christians, Muslims and Jews all believe Abraham showed a great example of faith in God.
  a. How did God test Abraham's faith?
  b. Was the test a fair one?
  c. How might you have responded if you had been in Abraham's place?

Extra activity

What happened in the past is very important to Jews today. What are the most important things in your past? In what ways have they helped to make you the person you are today?

Moses

Jacob, the grandson of Abraham, was given the name Israel and his descendants were known as 'the children of Israel' or 'Israelites'. They later came to be known as 'Jews'. A famine forced the Israelites to go to Egypt in search of food. To begin with the Egyptians treated them kindly but a new Pharoah made them his slaves.

The young Moses

The Israelites were slaves in Egypt for more than 400 years. Towards the end of this time, another Pharoah became alarmed that their numbers were growing so rapidly. He tried to kill them by ordering that all newborn Israelite boys should be thrown into the River Nile. One Israelite mother, however, hid her son, Moses, for three months before placing him in some bulrushes on the banks of the river. It was here that he was found by an Egyptian princess, who brought him up in the royal palace as if he was her own son.

Moses, the leader

Many years later God appeared to Moses and commanded him to go to the Pharoah to demand the release of the Israelite slaves. However, the Pharoah refused to let them go. To make the Pharoah change his mind, God sent ten plagues – the last one being the worst. After nine plagues had failed to change the Pharoah's mind, the Israelites were told by God to mark their door-posts with animal blood. That night the 'angel of death' killed the eldest son in every Egyptian household but passed over any house marked with blood. The Israelite children were safe.

The Pharoah let the Israelites leave Egypt but later changed his mind and gave chase. When they reached the Sea of Reeds (Red Sea), the waters parted and the Israelites were able to pass through

unharmed. The Egyptians, however, were swallowed up when the waters swept back. The escape from Egypt, known as the **Exodus**, is celebrated every year at the Jewish **Passover** festival. It is one of the most important events in their history.

The Ten Sayings

The journey from slavery, which took 40 years to complete, took the Israelites all the way back to Canaan (Israel). During this long journey through the wilderness they received the Torah from God. These books included the Ten Commandments, known by Jews as the Ten Sayings. These were written on tablets of stone and given to Moses by God on Mount Sinai. To remind Jews today of this important event, two tablets of wood, marble or stone are placed at the front of every synagogue (picture A). The beginning of each Saying is written on them in Hebrew.

Moses led the Israelites until they could see Canaan in the distance. Sadly, however, he died before they could reach it. It was left to Joshua to take them to their final destination.

A The Ten Sayings in stone or wood in every synagogue are a constant reminder of the importance of these laws

B Scrolls on which the Torah is written are kept in every synagogue

C A passage from the Torah is read during every Jewish act of worship

In the glossary

Exodus   Passover

Find the answers

- Why did Jacob and his family go to Egypt?
- What was the Exodus?
- Which laws were written on tablets of stone?

Learning about, learning from

1 a. Who was given the name 'Israel'?
  b. Where did the Israelites spend over 400 years in slavery and how did they leave?
  c. What is the journey of the Israelites from their time of slavery called?
  d. What did Moses receive from God on Mount Sinai?

2 Why do you think the festival of Passover is so called?

3 Read the Ten Sayings in Exodus 20.1–17. Imagine you belong to the new Jewish community. Make up ten laws of your own for this community. What would your laws try to achieve?

Extra activity

Many Jews believe that God's name is too holy to be spoken and so call him Adonai (Lord). God told Moses his name: 'I am who I am.' What do you think God meant by this?

Muhammad (1)

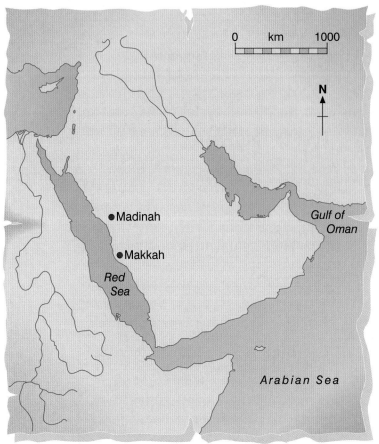

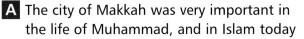

A The city of Makkah was very important in the life of Muhammad, and in Islam today

Muslims believe Allah has sent many prophets into the world, beginning with Adam and including Abraham and Jesus. Muhammad was the last, and the greatest, of Allah's prophets. At the age of 40 he experienced a series of revelations from Allah and these form the holy book, the Qur'an. Islam is now the major religion in many parts of the Middle East, Africa and the Far East.

The early life of Muhammad

Muhammad was born in the Arabian city of Makkah in 570 CE. At that time Makkah was at the centre of a prosperous caravan trade which ran between Arabia and the Mediterranean Sea (map A). The people who lived in Makkah worshipped many gods, believing their city to be holy.

Muhammad did not know his father. He died before Muhammad was born. When he was only six years old, his mother also died. His grandfather then looked after him, but he died two years after that. An orphan at an early age, Muhammad was brought up by his uncle, Abu Talib.

As an adult Muhammad worked as a camel driver and then as a trader. He soon built up a reputation for his honesty in business, earning himself the nickname of 'Al-Amin' – 'The Trustworthy One'.

Muhammad soon started to work for Khadijah, a rich widow who owned one of the camel trains. Although she was 15 years older than him, Khadijah asked Muhammad to marry her. During a long and happy marriage they had six children – four daughters and two sons. The two boys both died at a young age.

In Makkah

Muhammad was a very religious man. He spent a long time praying in the desert around Makkah and was upset by the behaviour of the people around him in the town. They worshipped many idols, which were made of stone, wood or clay and kept in or around the Ka'bah. The Ka'bah stood in the centre of Makkah, as it still does today. The people of Makkah believed that the Ka'bah was originally built by Ibrahim (Abraham), a prophet who had lived about 2500 years earlier. The holiest part of the Ka'bah was the Black Stone, given by the Angel Jibril (Gabriel) to Abraham.

One day heavy rain damaged the walls of the Ka'bah. They were soon repaired but the people argued over who should have the honour of putting the Black Stone back in place. As they could not come to an agreement, they decided that the first

B The city of Makkah was an important location on a prosperous camel trade route at the time of Muhammad

person to walk through the city the next morning would make the decision for them. That person was Muhammad. He told them to lay a cloak on the ground and to place the Black Stone on it. The four leaders of the tribes each took a corner of the cloak, and Muhammad guided the Black Stone back into position. The young man was greatly praised for his wisdom.

Find the answers

- In which parts of the world is Islam the main religion?

- Why was Makkah a particularly important city at the time of Muhammad?

- What is the Ka'bah?

Learning about, learning from

1 Answer these questions in your own words.
   a. Why did Muhammad have a sad childhood?
   b. Why was Muhammad greatly respected in his business dealings?
   c. What do we know about the marriage of Muhammad and Khadijah?

2 What did Muhammad think was wrong with the way the people lived in Makkah?

3 Muhammad spent much of his early life alone, thinking and praying in the desert. What do you think about when you are on your own? Why do you think this time was so important to Muhammad?

Extra activity

Why do you think that Muhammad's solution to replacing the Black Stone in the Ka'bah was particularly clever?

Muhammad (2)

Each year, during the month of **Ramadan**, Muhammad regularly spent time praying in a cave outside the city of Makkah. It was during his fifth visit to the cave that he had his first revelation from Allah.

The Angel Jibril

When he was 40 years old Muhammad began to receive visions of the Angel Jibril, an awesome heavenly being whose wings spread as far as the eye could see in every direction. The Angel told Muhammad three times to read and recite what he saw but he could neither read nor write. The Angel then squeezed him hard three times and Muhammed found that he could recite the words. You can read the English translation of these first words in the box on the next page.

Muhammad returned home quickly to tell his wife, who assured him that the revelation was from Allah and must be obeyed. Later revelations also followed and these convinced Muhammad that Allah would never abandon him. God would guide him in his mission as the final prophet and messenger of Allah. After his death his companions collected together all the revelations Muhammed had received from Allah to form the Muslim holy book, the Qur'an. Muslims believe that the Qur'an is the true word of Allah.

The Hijrah

Muhammad began to preach the message he had received to the people of Makkah. He insisted they should stop worshipping the 360 idols stored in the Ka'bah and, instead, start to worship the one true God, Allah. The people rejected his message. After years of trying to convince the people of Makkah, Muhammad left the city with some of his followers and travelled to **Madinah**. This journey, known as the **Hijrah**, took place in 622 CE and is the most important date in Islam. Ever since it has marked the beginning of the Islamic calendar, with 622 CE becoming the year 1 AH ('After Hijrah').

The people of Madinah welcomed the Prophet, as Muhammad was now known, and his companions warmly. He was made governor of the town and was able to put the new Islamic principles into practice there. Eight years later Muhammad returned to Makkah at the head of an army and conquered the city. He destroyed all the idols in the Ka'bah and cleansed the shrine before dedicating it to the true worship of Allah. The Ka'bah remains at the heart of Muslim worship today, with prayers being offered by worshippers throughout the world as they face towards the holy city (picture B).

Two years later, in 632 CE, Muhammad died. He had just completed a final pilgrimage to Makkah. Announcing his death to the people, Muhammad's friend Abu Bakr told them: 'Muhammad was a man. Muhammad is dead. God is alive, immortal.'

A These words at the front of a mosque remind Muslims that Allah alone is God and that Muhammad is His messenger

B A Muslim knows that as he prays in the **mihrab** in a mosque he is facing the holy city of Makkah

From the Qur'an

The Angel Jibril asked Muhammad to read these words:
In the Name of God, the Compassionate, the Merciful. Recite: In the Name of your Lord who created man from a clot of blood. Recite: And your Lord is Most Bountiful, who taught by the pen, taught man that which he did not know.

In the glossary

Hijrah   Mihrab
Madinah   Ramadan

Find the answers

- Which angel visited Muhammad?
- Into which book were the revelations collected?
- Which important event in Islam took place in 622 CE?

Learning about, learning from

1 Write down ten pieces of information you have found out about the Prophet Muhammad.

2 Three names for God are included in the quotation in the box.
   a. What are they?
   b. What do these names mean?

3 Why did Makkah, not Madinah, became the most holy city in Islam? How do Muslims everywhere show that they recognise this?

Extra activity

What do you think Abu Bakr really meant when he told the people: 'Muhammad was a man. Muhammad is dead. God is alive, immortal'? (Remember what Muhammad taught about worshipping idols.)

Guru Nanak (1)

The land of the five rivers in northern India is known as the Punjab – the word 'panj' means 'five'. Many people wanted to rule the Punjab as it was a good place to grow food and was a wealthy centre of trade. Invaders and traders shared their religious beliefs with those living in the area. In particular, the area was influenced by the old faith of Hinduism and the newer religion of Islam.

Early years

Guru Nanak (picture A) was born in 1469 CE in a village in the Punjab called Talwindi, close to the town of Lahore. He was the first of ten Gurus (teachers) who founded Sikhism. His birthplace is now known as Nankana Sahib and is in Pakistan. The birthday of Guru Nanak is celebrated by Sikhs each year in early November, the exact date being set by the time of the full moon.

A Guru Nanak, the founder of Sikhism

As with other great religious figures there are many stories about the birth and childhood of Guru Nanak. One of them tells of a dazzling white line around his head as he was born, which was noticed by the midwife. A local Hindu holy man foretold that the child was going to be a great man – maybe even a guru or 'wise man'. Guru Nanak's parents were Hindus and he was brought up in that faith.

At the age of 19 Guru Nanak's parents arranged for him to marry a Hindu woman and the couple had two children. He started work as an accountant for a Muslim family and this bought him, for the first time, into contact with many followers of Islam. The beliefs that he heard from them were very different from those of his Hindu upbringing. He discovered, in particular, that Muslims believe strongly in one God and this was to become the cornerstone of his own later religious beliefs.

A visit to heaven

Later, when he was 30, Guru Nanak disappeared whilst swimming in a local river and was feared to have drowned. Three days later, however, he reappeared to tell the villagers that he had visited heaven. In heaven he had been given **amrit** (nectar) to drink and had been told the name of the true God, Nam. He returned with a divine mission to teach men and women how to pray and meditate, to carry out deeds of love and charity and to live in a way that is pleasing to God. The most important belief, he said, is that all men are equal in the sight of God and this belief is at the heart of Sikhism.

In the glossary

Amrit

B Sikhs sit beneath a banner of Guru Nanak and Guru Gobind Singh, two highly respected Gurus

Guru Nanak's visit to heaven

This is how the Guru Granth Sahib, the Sikh holy book, describes the visit of Guru Nanak to heaven:

I was a minstrel out of work. The Lord gave me employment. The Mighty One instructed me: 'Night and day, sing my praise.' The Lord summoned the minstrel to his High Court. On me he bestowed the robe of honouring him and singing his praise. On me he bestowed the nectar in a cup, the nectar of his true and holy name.

Find the answers

- What did a holy man predict when Guru Nanak was born?

- When is Guru Nanak's birthday celebrated?

- How did the religions of Hinduism and Islam affect the early life of Guru Nanak?

Learning about, learning from

1 **a.** What does 'Punjab' mean?
   b. Where is the Punjab?
   c. Where was Guru Nanak born?
   d. What is the birthplace of Guru Nanak called now?

2 During his trip to heaven Guru Nanak learned that all people are equal in God's sight.
   a. Why did Guru Nanak place this lesson at the heart of his teaching?
   b. Make a list of the different groups you belong to, such as family, classes, teams or clubs. Is everyone treated equally in these groups?
   c. Can you think of an occasion that you have read or heard about when people were treated unfairly? What happened?
   d. Do you think everyone is equal?
   e. Would life be very different in the world today if people were to follow Guru Nanak's teaching?

Extra activity

When Guru Nanak was taken up into heaven he was given amrit to drink. Using books from the library and/or the internet, find out three pieces of information about amrit and the part it plays in Sikh worship.

Guru Nanak (2)

The visit that Guru Nanak paid to heaven changed the whole direction of his life. As a result, he gave up his work and became a travelling preacher. During the next 30 years he travelled the length and breadth of India and nearby countries on foot. A group of disciples soon gathered around him and these became the first Sikhs.

The travels of Guru Nanak

You can see from map A where Guru Nanak visited on his travels. He undertook four major journeys. He visited the Hindu holy places in the north-east, south and west of India, Sri Lanka and Tibet as well as the Muslim holy places of Makkah, Madinah and those in Iraq and Iran. Though most people he met could not read or write, they could learn the words of songs. So, on all his travels, he was accompanied by Mardana, a Muslim musician and a friend from childhood. When Mardana's father had tried to stop the two friends playing together, Guru Nanak told him: 'There's neither Hindu nor Muslim. We are all brothers.'

God is everywhere

Sikhs believe that Guru Nanak performed many miracles on his travels. He also encountered much opposition. On his visit to Makkah, a Muslim objected to him sleeping with his feet towards the Ka'bah. The man said this was disrespectful to Allah. Several times he moved Guru Nanak's feet, only to find that they still pointed towards the shrine. Nanak told him: 'God, Allah, is everywhere and is not found in any one place.'

In 1521 CE Guru Nanak founded a new town, Kartarpur ('the seat of God') so that people could visit him there to listen to his teachings. The Guru founded a community where his followers could work and worship together. He also started a kitchen, the **langar**, where free meals were served to all visitors. Everyone was involved in the preparation and serving of the food because everyone was equal. Such everyday work is not beneath the dignity of anyone. Gurdwaras today have a langar to continue this tradition. Free meals are provided at the end of every service.

Towards the end of his life, Guru Nanak chose Lehna, one of his most faithful companions, to succeed him. Lehna always tried to put the teachings of Guru Nanak into practice. On one occasion, as he was visiting the Guru, Lehna picked up a bundle of wet, muddy grass to help local villagers feed their cows. Guru Nanak's wife saw this and told her husband. Lehna was given the name Angad ('my limb'). By being prepared to help his fellow human beings in this way, Angad was showing that he understood the teachings of Guru Nanak. A few days later, on 22 September 1539, Guru Nanak died. Guru Angad took over the work of leading and teaching the growing Sikh community.

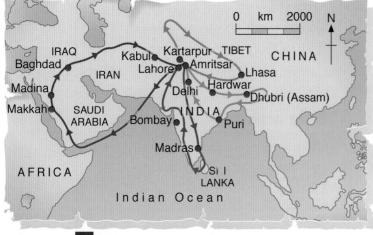

A This map shows the extensive travels of Guru Nanak after his visit to heaven

B Guru Gobind Singh, the tenth Guru, taught that there should be no hatred between religions

By Guru Nanak

Guru Nanak taught his followers:
It is through actions that some come nearer to God and some wander away.

In the glossary

Langar

Find the answers

- Which experience totally changed the direction of Guru Nanak's life?

- Where did Guru Nanak visit on his many travels?

- Who did Guru Nanak choose to succeed him and why?

Learning about, learning from

1 Why did Guru Nanak disagree with a Muslim over the direction in which his feet were pointing?

2 Why did Guru Nanak's friendship with Mardana cause problems to Mardana's father?

3 Guru Nanak taught that all people are equal and valuable in God's sight. Give one example of how Sikhs treat people to show they are following the Guru's teaching.

4 Do you agree with Guru Nanak that 'we are all brothers' – that what we have in common is more important than what makes us different? Explain your answer.

Extra activity

Guru Nanak insisted that all people, of whatever faith, were equal in the sight of God. Do you think it is possible that people from all religions are worshipping the same God, even if they do not realise it?

The Buddha (1)

The man that the followers of Buddhism call the Buddha (picture A) was born Siddhartha Gotama. He was born in about 563 BCE in the foothills of the Himalayas, near the present border between India and Nepal. His father ruled a local tribe, the Shakyas, and the young child was brought up in great luxury in a palace.

A Before he became the Buddha, Siddhartha Gotama spent a long time searching for the truth about suffering and life

Early years

Many legends have grown up around the birth of Siddhartha Gotama. There are stories of the whole earth being flooded with light when he was born; of the blind being able to see; of the lame walking and of prisoners' chains being snapped open. It is said that as soon as he was born the baby could walk seven steps and he was bathed in perfumed water by the gods.

Legend has it that before the birth of the child Gotama's father asked eight wise men what would become of his son in later life. They all agreed he would become a great ruler unless he saw the suffering around him, in which case he would be a great religious leader instead. Because he wanted his son to succeed him as ruler, his father tried to prevent him leaving the palace and seeing any suffering. When he was 16, Gotama married a beautiful wife and they had a son. Gotama named his son Rahula ('chains') because he felt that in spite of his life of luxury he himself was in chains. Life offered him no pleasure or happiness.

The Four Signs

Siddhartha Gotama was bored and frustrated by his sheltered life in the palace. One day, when he was 29 years old, he went riding in his chariot outside the palace and saw four things that disturbed him greatly. They also changed his life for ever. He saw:

- an old man about to die. From this Siddhartha Gotama realised that old age destroys a person's beauty and strength. He had never seen old age before.
- a sick person lying by the roadside. From this he saw for himself what sickness can do to a person. He had never seen sickness before.

B One of the people Siddhartha Gotama met when he left his palace was a Hindu holy man, who impressed him with his simple devotion to God

- a dead man being carried to a place of cremation. From this Siddhartha Gotama realised that everyone must die. He had never seen death before.
- a Hindu holy man, like the one in picture B, dressed in rags and owning nothing. Looking at the holy man he discovered that this person was truly happy because he was unafraid of suffering, old age and death.

The first three of these sights came as a great shock to Siddhartha Gotama. He realised that the problem of suffering went to the very heart of human life. Why do people suffer, grow old and die? Leaving his wife and child in the care of his family, Siddhartha Gotama set off to find the answers to these questions.

Find the answers

- When and where was Siddhartha Gotama born?
- What stories and legends are associated with his birth?
- Why did Siddhartha Gotama name his son Rahula?

Learning about, learning from

1 **a.** What were the four things that Siddhartha Gotama saw outside the palace?
   b. Why did they disturb him so much?

2 Imagine you are Siddhartha Gotama. Would you have wanted to see real life outside the palace or would you have settled for a life of luxury instead?

3 Parents often think they should protect their children from certain things in life.
   a. Describe two things your parents tried to protect you from until you were older.
   b. Describe two things you might try to protect your own children from.
   c. Do you think Siddhartha Gotama's parents were right to protect their son from suffering?

Extra activity

One of the legends associated with the birth of Siddhartha Gotama is that he was born out of the right side of his mother.
a. Why are legends often associated with the birth of great religious leaders?
b. Why is so much importance attached to the birth of these people?

The Buddha (2)

Siddhartha Gotama had been brought up in the Hindu faith, so he turned to this religion first to find an answer to suffering. He took off his royal clothes and cut his hair with a sword before living as a holy man for six years. He treated his body so harshly that he almost died – living for some time on just a single grain of rice a day. When he was close to death he realised that living like this was not the answer and that old age, suffering and death could not be avoided. They were facts of life which needed to be faced.

The Middle Way

Siddhartha Gotama had tried the way of luxurious living and the way of total self-denial, but neither of them had brought him true happiness or the answer to the problem of suffering. He decided to find a **Middle Way** between these two extremes. The five holy men who had shared their lives with him for the past six years left him and he sat beneath a fig tree vowing that he would not move until he found the answers to two questions:

- Why is there suffering in the world?
- Where is true happiness to be found?

Stories from the time tell us that Siddhartha Gotama was tempted by Mara, the force of darkness, to give up his search. He was also tempted by beautiful women and by a fear of the unknown to abandon his quest but he was determined to continue. He stayed beneath the tree all night, battling with the temptations.

Enlightenment

For a long time he sat in deep meditation in the lotus position. As you can see from picture B, this is a position that Buddhists use today when they meditate. By dawn Siddhartha Gotama had found the

A Buddhists present offerings to the Buddha to express their thankfulness to him for his willingness to help them to find enlightenment

answers to his questions and began to see the world as it really is – what Buddhists call 'enlightenment'. He saw both the cause of suffering and the way in which it can be ended. This was the moment when Siddhartha Gotama became the Buddha, the Enlightened One.

B Buddhists follow the example of the Buddha, who used meditation to help him find enlightenment

From a Buddhist holy book

How can there be laughter, when the whole world is burning? When you are in deep darkness, will you not ask for a lamp?

In the glossary

Middle Way

Find the answers

- Which religion was followed by Siddhartha Gotama's family?

- Why was the path of the Buddha called the Middle Way?

- What did Mara try to tempt Siddhartha Gotama to do?

Learning about, learning from

1 Draw six pictures to illustrate the most important events in the life of the Buddha. Write a sentence underneath each drawing to explain your pictures.

2 Think of some things that make it hard to concentrate totally on something. What things made it hard for Siddhartha Gotama to concentrate when he was trying to find the answer to the problem of suffering?

3 Looking at a statue of the Buddha is said to fill some people with a sense of peace. Look at the photographs of the Buddha on pages 36 and 37. Which things come into your mind?

4 Buddhists believe that death is always a part of life.
   a. What do they mean by this?
   b. Do you think we would all benefit if we were more aware of death when we are living?

Extra activity

The Buddha believed that old age, suffering and death are the most important facts of life that need to be faced. Which of these three frightens you the most? Explain your answer.

The Buddha (3)

According to the teachings of Buddhism, the Buddha could have left the earth for **nirvana** the moment he was enlightened. He chose not to do so. Convinced that his new insights must be taught to others, the Buddha spent the rest of his life teaching as a **bodhisattva** – a buddha who has reached enlightenment but who chooses to stay on earth to teach others.

Sarnath

After he was enlightened the Buddha went to a deer park in Sarnath where he explained to his friends about his new discoveries. He told them that he had found the answer to the problem of suffering and explained the **Four Noble Truths**:

A Although the Buddha could have left the earth after his enlightenment, he chose to remain behind to teach others

1 Everything in the world is **dukkha**, filled with bad as well as good things. The things we have done in life are called **karma** and these are carried forward from one life to the next. Buddhists believe in **reincarnation**, where people are born many times. Each time person is reborn they suffer for their actions in previous lives. As a result there is something imperfect about every new life.

2 Dukkha is caused by greed and selfishness. All humans are taken up with themselves and this causes suffering in the world. Even being reborn is selfish and people should try to break the cycle of birth and death.

3 Greed and selfishness can be ended. When people no longer crave for things, suffering can be stopped. Suffering and imperfection can be ended. It is only when people break out of cycle of birth and death that this can happen.

4 The way to stop selfishness and greed is to follow the Eight-Fold Path.

His four friends were so impressed by what the Buddha told them that they gave up their own search for the truth. They knew that the Buddha had already found it. They became the first Buddhists.

The Eight-Fold Path

Buddhism encourages people to follow the Middle Way between a life of luxury and one of total self-denial. The Eight-Fold Path is that Middle Way. People should:

- hold a right viewpoint (follow the teachings of Buddhism)
- have right thoughts (adopt an unselfish attitude to life)
- use right speech (avoid lies and gossip)
- live by right actions (avoid killing anything)
- follow a right livelihood (have an honest career)

- make the right effort (train themselves to do good)
- have the right awareness (gain control of the mind)
- have right concentration (become a calm person through meditation).

Parinirvana

The Buddha died at the age of 80. His body was cremated and the ashes were placed in special burial mounds called **stupas**. At the moment of death the Buddha reached parinirvana – the final and complete nirvana reached at the passing away of a Buddha.

B Nirvana, the state of secure, perfect peace, has been reached by the Buddha and Buddhists hope to attain it after many reincarnations

Crossing the ocean of suffering

After his enlightenment, the Buddha explained why he remained on earth: *Having crossed myself the ocean of suffering I must help others to cross it. Freed myself, I must set others free. This is the promise I have made in the past when I saw all that lives in distress.*

In the glossary

Bodhisattva	Nirvana
Dukkha	Reincarnation
Four Noble Truths	Stupas
Karma	

Find the answers

- What is a bodhisattva?
- What is a stupa?
- What is dukkha?

Learning about, learning from

1 Why did the Buddha not leave the earth as soon as he was enlightened?

2 **a.** Explain what the Buddha meant when he told his friends about the Middle Way.
   b. Why did he think the Middle Way was so important?

3 The Buddha taught that a person's occupation is important if they wish to reach enlightenment. Not only should they work hard but they should also work in a suitable career.
   a. What kind of jobs in today's world might he have considered unsuitable?
   b. What kind of jobs might be particularly suitable?

Extra activity

Why is training the mind as well as the body necessary for anyone who seeks to find the path to spiritual happiness? In which ways do you think you could 'train' your mind?

Jesus of Nazareth

Introduction

Nearly everything we know about Jesus, the founder of Christianity, comes from the **New Testament** in the Bible. The story of his birth, life, death and **resurrection** is told in the four **Gospels** at the beginning of the New Testament. Three of these accounts (Matthew, Mark and Luke) tell a similar story and share much of their information with each other. The fourth Gospel, John, is rather different to the others.

Jesus in the Gospels

Jesus was a Jew who was born in first-century Palestine when it was under Roman rule. Although we cannot be sure of the exact date of his birth, it was probably in either 4 or 5 BCE. Jews at the time were expecting a **Messiah** to be sent by God to save them from their enemies. Jesus said he was the Messiah but only a few people believed him at the time. This is because he was not the kind of Messiah they were expecting. He was not a military leader. He came to teach the people about God.

Christians believe that Jesus performed many miracles during his time on earth. Miracles, Christians say, prove that Jesus, as God's son, had control over the powers of nature, sickness and death. Jesus chose 12 men to be his travelling companions (disciples) and he taught them about God and his kingdom. To do this he used **parables**. The disciples continued the work of Jesus and set up the Christian Church after he had left the earth.

During his short life Jesus made many enemies, especially among the religious leaders. They persuaded the Roman authorities to arrest and try Jesus. Within a few hours of his arrest he was condemned to death by Pontius Pilate, a Roman governor, and crucified just outside the city of **Jerusalem**. Christians believe that Jesus was brought back to life by God after being dead for three days – an event known as the resurrection. The Christian faith is based on a belief in the life, death and resurrection of Jesus.

In this unit

In this unit you will read about the following:

- Apart from descriptions in the Gospels about the birth of Jesus, little is known about his childhood and early adulthood until he was baptised by John the Baptist in the River Jordan.

- Jesus performed many miracles by healing the sick and bringing the dead back to life – showing his control over the powers of nature.

- Jesus taught about God's kingdom using mainly parables and short, memorable stories.

- Towards the end of his life Jesus came to the city of Jerusalem on a donkey and drove the money changers out of the Temple.

- Jesus ate one last meal with his disciples, during which he taught them about his forthcoming death. The Christian celebration of **Holy Communion** is based on this meal.

- One of his disciples, Judas, betrayed him to the authorities.

- After two trials, Jesus was put to death by the Romans. He died by crucifixion on a hill outside the city of Jerusalem.

- Three days later, Christians believe Jesus rose from the dead. This event, known as the resurrection, is at the heart of the Christian faith.

In the glossary

Gospels	New Testament
Holy Communion	Parables
Jerusalem	Resurrection
Messiah	

Jesus in the Gospels

The Gospels show two sides to their picture of Jesus – the divine side and the human side. The idea of God being limited by human weakness is not easy to understand. Christians believe it is important, however, to understand both sides of Jesus.

The divine side

Jesus is the Son of God, showing all the power and authority you would expect God himself to show. The opening words of Mark's Gospel (see the box) reveal what the writer thought of Jesus. He demonstrated God-like powers and it was this that set him apart from other religious teachers of the time. He taught people with an authority that no one else had. He healed those who were ill and ordered demons out of those who were troubled by evil spirits. He walked on the waters of the Sea of Galilee and ordered the fierce winds and waves of the sea to be quiet. He knew what people were thinking without them saying a single word. There were times when even his closest friends were so overcome by what they saw they were speechless. The people were left in no doubt that this was God among them. Christians worship Jesus as God.

Before Jesus began to work in public he was baptised by John the Baptist in the River Jordan. As he was coming out of the water he saw the **Holy Spirit** and heard the voice of God from heaven. The voice told him that he was God's son and that God was pleased with him. From this moment, Jesus set about his work. He said he was going to set up God's kingdom in the hearts and minds of the people who were prepared to follow him. He told them they must put him before their homes and loved ones. Only God on earth could make such demands and expect people to respond.

The human side

The Gospel writers certainly treat Jesus as the Son of God, but they also show his human side. The same Jesus who showed power over sickness and evil was angry and impatient with the religious leaders and sometimes with his own friends and disciples, particularly **Peter**. We are told more than once that he was hungry and thirsty. This was especially true when he was tempted by the devil in the wilderness in the days following his baptism. Jesus was filled with pity and sadness when a leper came to him without anyone to help him. It was this strong feeling of love which led him to perform miracles. He was overcome with sadness when God and his friends seemed to desert him at the end of his life when he was in the greatest need.

A This icon seems to suggest the divine side of Jesus, with his fingers lifted to bless those who come to him in need

WHERE I AM THERE SHALL ALSO MY SERVANT BE

B In this statue we see a weaker, more human side of Jesus – this is the one we see most often in the Gospels

From Mark's Gospel

Mark opened his Gospel with these words:
This is the Good News about Jesus Christ, the Son of God.

In the glossary

Holy Spirit   Peter

Find the answers

- Which two sides of Jesus do we see in the Gospels?

- What set Jesus apart from other religious teachers at the time he was living?

- Who baptised Jesus?

Learning about, learning from

1 **a.** Give two examples of how the Gospels tell us that Jesus was God.
   b. Give two examples of how the Gospels show us that Jesus was a human person.

2 The Gospels give us two very different sides to the character and personality of Jesus. What did the Gospel writers want their readers to learn from their writings?

3 Some people may think that some things said about Jesus in the Gospels might be better left unsaid – that he was angry, impatient, disappointed, etc. Do you think it would be better if we did not know these things?

Extra activity

People have looked for many years for proof that the events in the Gospels actually happened. If we were to find conclusive proof that Jesus lived and died as the Gospels describe, would you then be convinced he was the Son of God? Do you think it matters either way?

The early life of Jesus

The only records that we have of the birth of Jesus are found in two of the Gospels, those of Matthew and Luke. Both agree that Jesus was born in the tiny Palestinian village of Bethlehem in a stable.

The birth of Jesus

Matthew's Gospel tells us that the conception of Jesus was first announced by an angel to Joseph. Joseph and Mary, Jesus's mother, were not married – although they had agreed to marry. Normally, in these circumstances, Joseph would have broken off the agreement. The angel, knowing this, told Joseph that the baby had been conceived by God's Holy Spirit and not by any human father.

In Luke's Gospel the birth of Jesus was announced to Mary, not Joseph. Mary was deeply worried by the news that she was to give birth to 'the Christ' (the Messiah). Jesus was God's son. She was assured that God was the father of her baby and not Joseph. Mary's song of praise after she received the news is called the 'Magnificat'. It is a psalm which is sung in many church services.

Early visitors

The birth of Jesus took place in a stable in Bethlehem. His name means 'God saves'. Luke's Gospel explains that the first visitors to the new baby were some shepherds. Matthew, however, does not mention the shepherds. Instead, he concentrates on a group of Magi (stargazers) who brought gifts of gold, frankincense and myrrh to the child and his parents. Whilst the shepherds were Jewish visitors, the Magi were not. They were Gentiles (non-Jews). This was to show that Jesus had come to help everyone in need – Jews and Gentiles alike.

Jesus grows up

Shortly after these events the Gospels fall silent. We know that as a Jewish child Jesus will have undergone **circumcision** eight days after being born and will have been educated in the local synagogue school between the ages of 5 and 13. Learning the Jewish scriptures by heart would have formed an important part of this education.

Jesus's parents would not have taken him with them when they visited the Temple in Jerusalem for the Passover festival each year. They did, however, take him for the first time when he was 12 years old. Judaism teaches that at this age a boy becomes an adult, responsible for his own religious behaviour. After the festival Mary and Joseph set off for home with their friends and relations. They thought that Jesus was with the party but soon discovered he had been left behind. They quickly returned to Jerusalem but it took them three days to find him.

Jesus had been talking and arguing with religious leaders in the Temple. He told his parents that he had come to earth to do the will of his Father in heaven.

A A crib in a church announces that the festival of Christmas is drawing close

B Jesus was brought up by Mary and Joseph, although Christians have always recognised that he was God's son

C As far as we know, Jesus had a perfectly normal Jewish upbringing

In the glossary

Circumcision

Find the answers

- What is the name of Mary's 'song of praise' after she learned she was to give birth to God's son?

- What does the name 'Jesus' mean?

- For which Jewish festival did Jesus go to the Temple with his parents?

Learning about, learning from

1 a. According to Matthew's Gospel, who first received the news that God's son was to be born?
   b. In Luke's Gospel, who was the first to be told that Jesus was to be born?
   c. Who were the Magi and what gifts did they bring to Jesus?
   d. Why was the visit of the Magi to Jesus particularly important?

2 Do you think the story of Jesus's birth is how Jews of the time expected the Messiah to come to earth?

3 Read the story of Jesus in the Temple again. Which things in the story show Jesus to be the Son of God, and which things show him to be human?

Extra activity

What do you think Jesus was really telling his parents when he said he had come to earth to do God's work?

The teachings of Jesus

The Gospels are full of the teachings of Jesus. Mark's Gospel tells us the first thing Jesus that told the people: 'The time has come – the kingdom of God is close.' Most of the teachings of Jesus were about the kingdom of God.

The kingdom of God

When he spoke about the kingdom of God, Jesus was speaking about God's rule and authority. He was not speaking about a kingdom, a country or a place. He was speaking about God ruling in the hearts and lives of men and women. He spoke about the rule of God as something that had come and was yet to come. People listening to Jesus could respond to God's kingdom even as they listened. Some time in the future, however, Jesus would return to set up God's kingdom on earth.

Parables

One of Jesus's favourite teaching methods was by using parables – stories with a religious meaning. Jesus left his listeners to work out the message behind the story. The parables of Jesus were particularly popular because he used ordinary things and everyday situations that the people could understand. Here are two examples:

- Picture B illustrates one parable of Jesus. He spoke of a shepherd who had 100 sheep to look after but lost one of them. Sheep on the hillsides of Palestine were a familiar sight. Penning up the rest for safety, the shepherd went in search of the missing sheep and was overjoyed when he found it. The parable means that God had sent Jesus into the world to help those people who had lost their way in life.
- You can read another parable in the box on the next page. This story again used a familiar sight in Palestine. A sower scattered his seed on to the soil. Some

of the soil was fertile and yielded a good harvest, while other soil was barren and the seed was wasted. The message behind this parable is that when Jesus told the people about God's kingdom, some of them responded. However, the message was wasted on others.

The Sermon on the Mount

The parables of Jesus are found throughout the Gospels. However, Matthew gathered many of them together, along with some other teachings of Jesus, into the Sermon on the Mount. The main message of the Sermon is that people should not make an outward show of their devotion to God. Those who do so are called 'hypocrites' as they simply want to be praised by others. Other people may admire them, but God does not. A person's devotion to God can only be shown by the kind of life they lead. They will live peaceably, humbly, put the

A Jesus was most remembered for the authority of his teaching

interests of others before their own and pray to God in the privacy of their own home. If they do this and try only to please God, they will find that God rewards them openly.

B The parable of the lost sheep was one of the most memorable stories that Jesus told

Find the answers

- What is a parable?

- What was the message of the parable of the lost sheep?

- From where did Jesus mostly take the examples for his parables?

The sower and the seed

A farmer went out to sow his seed. As he was scattering the seed, some fell along the path, and the birds came and ate it all up. Some fell on rocky places, where there was not much soil. It sprang up quickly because the soil was shallow. But when the sun came up, the plants were scorched and they withered because they had no roots. Other seed fell among thorns, which grew up and choked the plants so that they did not bear grain. Other seed fell on good soil. It came up, grew and produced a crop multiplying 30, 60 or even 100 times.

Learning about, learning from

1 Why did Jesus teach people mainly through the use of parables?

2 Read the parable of the sower and the seed in the box above. What was Jesus trying to teach people by telling this parable? Check your answer with the explanation that Mark gives in 4.13–20.

3 **a.** What is a hypocrite?
   b. Why was Jesus particularly hard on hypocrites?
   c. If Jesus was on earth today, what kind of people do you think he might be particularly critical of?

4 Make up your own parable to explain how you think people should behave towards others. Remember to use ordinary things and everyday situations to explain what you mean.

Extra activity

People respond differently to the message of a religion. What kinds of things do you think might affect whether someone is religious or not?

The miracles of Jesus

At first, Jesus was greeted enthusiastically by people wherever he went. One of the first things he did was to choose 12 disciples. These were men from all walks of life that Jesus would teach and trust to continue with his work after he had left the earth. Among these disciples were Peter and Judas. Peter was later to deny that he even knew Jesus, while Judas betrayed him to the authorities.

The miracles of Jesus

Apart from the teachings of Jesus, the other remarkable feature of his life was the miracles the Gospels say he performed. A miracle is an event which seems to be outside the laws of nature. To the writers of the Gospels, these miracles demonstrated that Jesus was God. Ordinary people simply do not have that

kind of power. The Gospels tell us that Jesus:

- restored sight to many people who were blind and hearing to the deaf
- cured those who were dumb
- healed those suffering from various illnesses and diseases, including leprosy
- raised people from the dead – we are told that he brought a young girl (picture A), and a friend, Lazarus (picture B), back to life
- calmed a raging storm
- turned water into wine
- walked on water without sinking
- fed a large crowd using just five loaves and two fish.

There are many other miracles in the Gospels. Sometimes Jesus seemed to have healed people because he was upset by what he saw. Often he used his power over nature to show his disciples that he was God's Son. More than once he performed a miracle to test someone's faith.

In public and private

Miracles, however, are not the only things we learn about Jesus from the Gospels. We know that he spent much time teaching his disciples but he also entered into heated arguments with the Jewish religious authorities. They were not prepared to accept his authority or see him as God's Son. They certainly did not believe he was God's chosen Messiah. He also spent time blessing children who were brought to him and using them to teach people important spiritual truths (picture C).

We can also learn about the private side of Jesus in the Gospels. He often withdrew from the public eye to pray and think in the desert or on a mountainside. He needed time to be alone with himself and with God.

A On one occasion Jesus brought a young girl back to life

 Jesus brought Lazarus back to life after he had been dead for some time. The power to do this was thought to show that Jesus was the Son of God

 Jesus taught his listeners that they needed to become like little children if they were to enter God's kingdom

 Find the answers

- What is a miracle?

- Which disciple denied Jesus and which one betrayed him?

- Why did Jesus perform miracles?

Learning about, learning from

1 Make a list of three different types of miracles that Jesus performed.

2 **a.** Do you ever try to spend some time on your own? Why is this time important to you?
 b. Why did Jesus need a private side to his life, when he withdrew from people and spent time on his own? What do you think he might have gained from these times?

3 **a.** Why did Jesus chose a group of friends, or disciples, who would be with him constantly?
 b. What do you think his disciples might have learned from him?
 c. What do you think Jesus expected of them?

Extra activity

Do you think miracles really happened in the time of Jesus? Can they happen today?

The last week

As he neared the end of his life, Jesus worked his way towards the city of Jerusalem. He arrived on the outskirts of the city just before the Jewish festival of Passover was about to start. Pilgrims travelled from all over the Roman Empire to be there at this time of the year. Most of them travelled on foot but Jesus chose another way to enter the city.

Into Jerusalem

Centuries earlier the Jewish prophet, Zechariah, had spoken of the time when Israel's future king, the Messiah, would enter Jerusalem riding on a donkey (see the box on the next page). When Jesus rode into Jerusalem on a donkey he received a warm welcome from his disciples as well as from some of the city's inhabitants. They threw their cloaks on the road in front of him and shouted 'Hosanna'. They were welcoming Jesus as their king.

On the next day, however, the mood of the people changed completely. It happened after Jesus had entered the Temple and driven out the money changers who worked there. He was angry that they had turned the building, God's house, into a marketplace.

The betrayal

Before Jesus arrived in Jerusalem Judas, one of his disciples, had approached the Jewish leaders. He had offered to betray Jesus to them for 30 pieces of silver – the wages of a labourer in Jerusalem for about four months' work. The authorities were delighted with his offer. They knew that if they arrested Jesus openly the people might well have rebelled. Now, with the help of one of his disciples, they could take Jesus quietly and avoid any trouble with the crowd.

One last meal

A day or so later, Jesus sat down to eat one last meal with his disciples (picture B). It was the night before the Passover festival was due to begin and he used the occasion to tell his disciples that one of the group would betray him. He said:

> The Son of Man [Jesus] will go just as it is written about him. But woe to that man who betrays the Son of Man! It would be better for him if he had never been born.

Jesus then told his disciples that he was going to die. He used two items on the table to explain what would happen, so that his disciples would remember him:

- The loaf of bread, which he broke in front of them to show that his own body would be broken on the cross.
- The goblet of wine, which he used to speak of his blood being spilt.

A Shortly before he died, a woman washed the feet of Jesus with precious ointment and then wiped them with her hair. She did this to express her love for him

This meal is called the **Last Supper**. For centuries Christians have remembered this occasion, and the death and resurrection of Jesus, by eating bread and drinking wine at the service of Holy Communion or the **Mass**. Only two groups of Christians – the Salvation Army and the Quakers – do not celebrate this service.

B During the Last Supper Jesus suggested to his disciples that they should remember him after his death

A king riding on a donkey

These words were spoken by the prophet Zechariah in the Old Testament:

Rejoice, greatly, O Daughter of Zion! Shout, Daughter of Jerusalem! See, your king comes to you, righteous, and having salvation, gentle, and riding on a donkey. On a colt, the foal of a donkey.

In the glossary

Last Supper   Mass

Find the answers

- Why did Jesus enter Jerusalem on a donkey?
- What did Jesus do when he entered the Temple?
- How did Jesus make it possible for his followers to remember him?

Learning about, learning from

1 **a.** Who betrayed Jesus?
   b. Who did he betray Jesus to?
   c. What was he given in return for his betrayal?

2 Seeing the money lenders in the Temple clearly upset Jesus. People had to pay some money to the Temple, and to do this they had to change their Roman money into Jewish coinage. The money lenders in the Temple charged heavy interest on this. Why do you think this made Jesus angry?

3 The symbols of bread and wine have come to mean a great deal to Christians through their celebration of Holy Communion. Can you think of any other symbols which have become important for Christians today? What are they and what do they mean?

 ## Extra activity

Read the quotation in the box. It highlights two very different aspects of the personality of the Messiah, Jesus. What are they?

Jesus's death

For some time, opposition to Jesus had been growing steadily. All the religious leaders agreed that Jesus must be arrested, tried and put to death as soon as possible. This was the only way to put an end to his power over the people. So it was that the Temple guards, led by Judas, arrested Jesus. In a short period of time Jesus was taken before each of the following:

- Annas, the father-in-law of the High Priest, Caiaphas. Annas had once been High Priest himself and was curious to find out more about Jesus.
- Caiaphas, the High Priest. Caiaphas asked Jesus whether he was the Son of God. He replied: 'The words are yours.' Caiaphas took this to be **blasphemy** and tore his own clothes in front of everyone, a Jewish sign of great grief.

- The **Sanhedrin**, the Jewish Council, which met shortly after dawn. They asked Jesus the same question as Caiaphas. Jesus told them that he was the Messiah and they found him guilty of blasphemy. The Sanhedrin, however, did not have the authority to condemn a person to death. Only Pontius Pilate, the Roman governor, could do that.
- Pontius Pilate, who could not condemn Jesus to death for being found guilty of blasphemy. Jesus's enemies, therefore, accused him of other crimes, such as:
  - misleading the Jewish people
  - telling the people not to pay their taxes to the Romans
  - claiming to be the Messiah who would lead the people against the Romans.

Pilate questioned Jesus but he could find no reason to punish him. An old custom allowed him to release a prisoner at festival time and he offered to let Jesus go – but the crowd demanded the release of Barabbas, a thief and a murderer (see the box on the next page). Pilate asked Jesus a direct question: 'Are you the King of the Jews?' to which Jesus replied: 'The words are yours.' No Roman law had been broken yet the crowd persuaded Pilate to condemn Jesus to death. They reminded him that, if he let Jesus go, the authorities in Rome might decide he was a weak ruler, which could mean the end of his career and his life.

Giving in to public pressure, Pilate handed Jesus over to his soldiers. They dressed him in a purple robe and put a crown of thorns on his head. They beat him with a cane that resembled the sceptre of a king.

A This banner illustrates some of the events in the last few hours of the life of Jesus

The end

So, Jesus was crucified. A notice was nailed to his cross saying: 'Jesus of Nazareth, King of the Jews.' The Jewish leaders asked Pilate to change its wording but he refused. He replied: 'What I have written, I have written.' Otherwise, both the Jews and the Romans were satisfied. While he was dying Jesus felt deserted by everyone, including his disciples and God. Within six hours he was dead. The Gospel writers say that his last words were simply: 'It is finished.'

B After Jesus was condemned, he began to carry his cross to the place of crucifixion but collapsed under its weight

Pilate's offer

The chief priests and elders persuaded the crowd to ask Pilate to set Barabbas free and have Jesus put to death. But Pilate asked the crowd: 'Which of these two do you want me to set free for you?' 'Barabbas,' they answered. 'What, then, shall I do with Jesus called the Messiah?' Pilate asked them. 'Crucify him,' they all answered.

In the glossary

Blasphemy   Sanhedrin

Find the answers

- Which Jewish Council condemned Jesus?
- What is blasphemy?
- What was written above the head of Jesus when he was crucified?

Learning about, learning from

1 Explain why you think the Jewish authorities condemned Jesus.

2 Pilate felt Jesus did not deserve to die but he was also worried about damaging his career if he was seen to be lenient. Imagine you are one of Jesus's friends. Write a letter complaining about Pilate to his boss. What arguments would you use to demand his resignation?

3 Some Christian pilgrims go to Jerusalem to retrace the final steps of Jesus from the place where he was tried by Pilate to the place of his crucifixion. Why do they choose to do this, and what do you think they might gain from making the pilgrimage?

Extra activity

If Jesus was the Son of God it would have been easy for him to escape crucifixion. For Christians, however, the fact that he suffered and died as a human being is incredibly important. Why do you think this is?

After death

At the time of Jesus only the very wealthy could afford to have their own private tombs, which were often carved out of the hillside. They were sealed by a large stone, which was rolled out of the way to gain entrance. Inside there was a stairway that led to an underground burial chamber. Another low opening often led to a second chamber. The tomb in which the body of Jesus was laid would have been like this.

The burial of Jesus

The usual fate of a crucified person in Jerusalem was to be thrown into a burning pit outside the city. This would have happened to the body of Jesus had it not been for an important Jewish leader, Joseph of Arithmathea. He asked for Pilate's permission to lay the body of Jesus in the tomb he had built for himself.

There was some real urgency to the request. It was late Friday afternoon when Jesus died and the Jewish **Sabbath Day** was about to begin. Jewish law ruled out any work being done on the Sabbath Day. In the case of Jesus, there was not even enough time to anoint his body with spices – a job usually done by female relatives or friends. Instead, it was wrapped hurriedly in a linen cloth and laid on a ledge in the tomb.

Sunday

Early on the Sunday morning some female friends of Jesus went to the tomb to anoint his body properly. They were amazed to find the stone rolled away from the entrance and the tomb empty. Inside they found two angels dressed in white, waiting to greet them with the words: 'He is not here; he has been raised' (see the box on the next page). The women were terrified and ran away.

The women ran to tell the disciples exactly what they had seen. Peter and John ran to the tomb to see for themselves whether their story could be true. They found the tomb empty but, when John saw that the cloth and head-covering had not been disturbed, he believed that Jesus had come back to life. Peter was less sure. In the following days, however, Jesus appeared to his disciples, and to others, more than once. He left none of them in any doubt that he was alive. The belief that Jesus came back to life – the resurrection – is at the heart of the Christian faith.

After the resurrection

The Gospels describe the events of the resurrection in their own ways. They were written many years after these events took place and so a little confusion is understandable. Nevertheless, for more than 2000 years the Christian Church has preached the message that Jesus was put to death and, three days later, rose from the dead. This is the event which the Church throughout the world celebrates each year at **Easter**.

A The resurrection is the most important event in the Christian Church

B Christians believe that, 40 days after the resurrection, Jesus left the earth for the last time

Jesus is alive

The angels in the tomb told this message to the women on the first Easter morning:

Why are you looking among the dead for one who is alive? He is not here; he has been raised. Remember what he said to you while he was in Galilee: 'The Son of Man must be handed over to sinners, be crucified, and three days later rise to life.'

In the glossary

Easter   Sabbath Day

 Find the answers

- Who was Joseph of Arithmathea?
- Why was there a real need to bury the body of Jesus quickly?
- What do the Gospels say happened at the tomb on the Sunday morning?

Learning about, learning from

1 a. When do Christians believe Jesus was raised from the dead?
   b. Who were the first people to be told about Jesus rising from the dead?
   c. What did they do next?
   d. What did John and Peter do?

2 Do you find it surprising that the Gospels tell the story of the resurrection in different ways? What reasons could there be for these differences, and do they matter?

3 Imagine you are one of Jesus's disciples. Describe your feelings when you first hear that he has risen from the dead. Do you believe the first report or not?

Extra activity

The most important symbol of Christianity is the cross. Sometimes crosses are shown with the body of Jesus on them and sometimes they are empty. What do you think these two kinds of cross symbolise?

Religious buildings

Introduction

Many of the world's most beautiful buildings have been dedicated to the worship of God. Among them are Westminster Abbey and York Minster in Britain, the Sikh **Golden Temple** in **Amritsar** and the Dome of the Rock in Jerusalem.

Houses of God

People have worshipped God long before they built special buildings for that purpose. Jews, for example, have not always worshipped in synagogues. During the time of Moses they worshipped God in portable temples called Tabernacles. The early Christians met together in each other's homes for almost 300 years before the first churches were built.

However, the time came when special buildings became necessary so that worshippers could meet together and pray in privacy. These buildings were dedicated to the worship of God and this made them special. To people who came to them to pray and praise they were considered to be 'holy ground'. The behaviour of those who went inside to worship was expected to be special and different. It is still the same today. Worshippers may be expected to take off their shoes, wash themselves in running water or bow in front of the **altar** as they enter. Special actions are expected because they are entering a special place, the presence of God.

In most places of worship there is a focal point to which the worshipper's attention is immediately drawn. In a church this is the altar or **pulpit**; in a synagogue it is the **Ark**, where the scrolls of the Torah are kept; in a gurdwara it is the Sikh holy book itself, the Guru Granth Sahib.

Many religious buildings are also used as community centres where people can meet. Synagogues, for example, are Jewish places of learning where young and old come together to learn about and discuss their religious faith. In recent years many Muslims and Sikhs have moved to Britain from their country of birth. Mosques and gurdwaras are often used to prepare them for their new lives.

In this unit

In this unit you will read about the following:

- In Anglican, Roman Catholic and Orthodox churches the altar is the focal point from where services are conducted. The **font** is placed just inside the door and there are statues or **icons** in many of these churches.

- In Nonconformist churches the pulpit is the central feature. Preaching the Bible from the pulpit is the most important part of a Nonconformist service.

- The Ark, containing the scrolls of the Torah, dominates the inside of a synagogue. A plaque showing the Ten Commandments is visible on the wall.

- Mosques are often simple buildings containing little apart from a minbar – a portable platform. The mihrab – a niche in the wall – indicates the direction of the holy city of Makkah.

- The inside of a gurdwara is dominated by the **takht**, the throne on which the Guru Granth Sahib is placed. Outside, a flag shows that the building is a gurdwara. A langar – a free kitchen – can be found in every gurdwara.

- Statues of the gods and goddesses can be seen inside a Hindu mandir. Offerings are placed in front of the statues as a part of worship.

- There are many images of the Buddha in a Buddhist shrine. Offerings are placed in front of them as a way of paying homage.

In the glossary

Altar	Font	Pulpit
Amritsar	Golden Temple	Takht
Ark	Icons	

From an old Hindu text

The best places for worship are holy grounds, river banks, caves, sites of pilgrimages, the summits of mountains, confluences of rivers, sacred forests, solitary groves, the shade of the bel tree, valleys, places overgrown with tulsi plants, pasture lands, cow sheds, island sanctuaries, the shore of the sea, one's own house, the abode of one's teacher, places which tend to inspire single-pointedness, lonely places free from animals.

Churches (1)

There are almost 50,000 churches in Britain. Nearly half of these belong to the **Church of England** (Anglican Church). The most important of these churches are cathedrals, over which a **bishop** presides. Roman Catholics also have their own cathedrals, bishops, churches and priests. There are far fewer Orthodox churches in Britain.

Church of England churches

Church of England buildings are called parish churches. This is because the Church divides the whole country into 'parishes', with every person in Britain being served by a church. Most parish churches have a **vicar** to conduct their services. In the Church of England the vicar can be either a man or a woman.

The focal point of a Church of England church is the altar, which is usually at the eastern end of the building. Candles, a cross and perhaps an open Bible may be found on the altar. People kneel in front of the altar to receive the bread and wine during Holy Communion. Both the **lectern**, from where Bible passages are read, and the pulpit, from where the sermon is preached, stand between the worshippers and the altar.

The font stands just inside the door of the church. This holds the water for **infant baptism**. Some Christians believe that a baby becomes a member of the Church through baptism. Babies are baptised when they are a few months old.

Roman Catholic churches

Church of England and Roman Catholic churches often look similar inside – with their altars, lecterns, pulpits and fonts – but there are some important differences. There are likely to be more candles on a Catholic altar, as well as a **crucifix** – a cross bearing the body of Jesus. However, you may sometimes find these in Anglican churches too.

You will also see one or more statues of the **Virgin Mary** in a Catholic church and there is often one outside the church as well. Somewhere in a Catholic church there will be a candelabra holding many small candles. Worshippers who come may light a candle before they pray. In many Catholic churches there is also a small cubicle where people sometimes go to confess their sins to the priest.

Orthodox churches

The dome of an Orthodox church reminds people of the heaven stretched over the earth. The square shape shows that all people are equal in the sight of God. The four corners of the church are a reminder that people come from all corners of the earth to worship God. The **iconostasis** – a screen covered with icons – stands in front of the altar and only the priest is allowed through this when he is conducting the service of the **Holy Liturgy**.

A In Anglican and Roman Catholic churches worship takes place around the altar

B There are more Church of England churches than any other churches in Britain

C A Roman Catholic church. In many ways, a Roman Catholic church is similar to an Anglican church but you will notice some differences if you look carefully

In the glossary

Bishop	Infant baptism
Church of England	Lectern
Crucifix	Vicar
Holy Liturgy	Virgin Mary
Iconostasis	

Find the answers

- Which Church has more churches than any other in Britain?

- Where in a church do worshippers receive the bread and wine when taking Holy Communion?

- What is an iconostasis?

Learning about, learning from

1 Write down what each of the following are used for in an Anglican or Roman Catholic church.
   a. Lectern.
   b. Pulpit.
   c. Altar.
   d. Font.

2 How might you recognise:
   a. The inside of an Anglican church?
   b. The inside of a Roman Catholic church?

3 Imagine you have just paid a visit to an empty church. Write a poem to describe what you saw and how you felt as you sat and looked around.

Extra activity

In many modern church buildings the altar is placed in the middle of the church with the people gathered around it. What does this sort of design say about the Church?

Churches (2)

Nonconformists are Christians who do not belong to the Anglican, Roman Catholic or **Orthodox Church**. There are many **Nonconformist Churches** in Britain, including Methodists, Baptists, Salvation Army and Quakers. They may call their places of worship churches, chapels, citadels or meeting houses. The main feature of all these buildings, however, is that they are plain and simple, and this makes them different from many other churches and cathedrals.

Methodist and Baptist churches

In Anglican and Roman Catholic churches, the altar is the centre of worship. In Methodist or Baptist churches (picture B), the pulpit is at the heart of worship. It is from there that the Bible is explained and preached. There is no altar in a Nonconformist church. Instead, there is usually a communion table at the front where the bread and wine are laid out for the service of Breaking of Bread or the Lord's Supper – Holy Communion.

Baptist churches baptise adults, not infants, so there is no font inside these buildings. Instead, there is a baptismal pool at the front of the building. This is filled with water for the special service of **believer's baptism**. Occasionally, however, adults are baptised in a nearby river or the sea.

Citadels

The Salvation Army calls its places of worship 'citadels' (a citadel is a place of refuge). The band sits on the upper level to lead the people in their worship (picture C). At the front of this is a ledge from where an officer leads the worship. The worshippers sit on the lower level. The mercy seat is a long bench in front of the congregation. Anyone can come forward during a service and kneel at this bench if they want to ask God's forgiveness or simply wish to pray. Salvation Army citadels also display the special flag of the movement – the only Church to do so – together with the distinctive Army crest.

Meeting houses

The Quakers have a different style of worship to other Nonconformists, which is reflected in their places of worship (picture A). These meeting houses are very simple – there are no altars, pulpits, fonts or lecterns. People gather around a central table, which might have flowers and an open Bible on it. Quaker services are essentially silent, with each person reflecting on his or her own relationship with God.

A Quaker meeting houses are places where worshippers meet to offer God a largely silent form of worship

B The pulpit, from where the Bible is preached, forms the focal point in both Methodist and Baptist churches

C Worshippers in a Salvation Army citadel sometimes come forward to confess their sins at the mercy seat

In the glossary

Believer's baptism
Nonconformist Churches
Orthodox Church

 Find the answers

- Who are Nonconformists?
- What is the focal point in a Methodist or Baptist church?
- What are citadels and meeting houses?

 Learning about, learning from

1 **a.** Name three Nonconformist Churches.
   b. What are two names used in Nonconformist Churches for the service of Holy Communion?
   c. What takes place at the communion table in a Methodist church?

2 The Salvation Army calls its places of worship 'citadels'. What does the word mean and why do you think they have been given this name?

3 **a.** Would you rather be forgiven for something you had done wrong in private or in front of others?
   b. What do members of the Salvation Army use the mercy seat for? Why is it used in this way?

Extra activity

Which form of worship appeals to you most – one that has noise, colour and splendour or one that is very simple and peaceful? Explain your answer.

Synagogues

The most important acts of Jewish worship take place at home but worship in a synagogue is also important. The word 'synagogue' means 'coming together' and this is just what happens there. It is a place where Jews come together – to pray, worship, study, learn and relax. It is also the community centre for Jews, where important family events such as **bar mitzvahs** and weddings are celebrated. Many modern Jews prefer to call the synagogue by its more familiar name, shul.

Inside a synagogue

Inside a synagogue, in front of the eastern wall and facing the holy city of Jerusalem, stands the Ark. This is covered by heavy curtains and holds the scrolls of the Torah, the most important part of the Jewish scriptures. These scrolls are taken out of the Ark each time they are read in a service. While they stand in the Ark they are 'dressed' in special covers.

Two tablets of wood or stone can be found on the wall close to the Ark. The first few words of the Ten Commandments are written on them in Hebrew. The Jewish scriptures tell us that when these commandments were first given by God to Moses on Mount Sinai, they were written on tablets of stone. The Ten Commandments are very important to Jews because they explain what God expects of them.

Above the Ark a light always burns – this is called the ner tamid ('everlasting light'). It reminds Jews of the light that always

A In this synagogue you can see the balcony where women and children sit for worship

B In a synagogue Jews come together to worship, study and pray

Find the answers

- What does the word 'synagogue' mean?

- What is kept in the Ark?

- Why is a light is always kept burning above the Ark?

burned in the Temple in Jerusalem many centuries ago, as well as reassuring them that God is always with them today.

Reading the Torah

During each service in the synagogue on the Sabbath Day, and on special festival days, a scroll – called the Sefer Torah – is taken out of the Ark. It is carried in procession to the bimah – a platform at the front of the synagogue – where it is spread out. A man is usually chosen to read from the scroll although, in some cases, a woman can be given this honour. The bimah is a raised platform, so the person reading is said to 'go up' to the Torah. This shows that God's Word, the Torah, is higher than any human being. The people in the congregation 'sit beneath' the Torah, indicating that the holy book, and its teaching, has authority over them.

In most synagogues men and women sit separately. Women, girls and young children sit together in the balcony, while the men and older boys sit on the ground floor. In some synagogues, called Liberal or Reform synagogues, families sit together for worship.

Learning about, learning from

1 a. What is the Ark in a synagogue?
  b. Why is the Ark such an important part of a synagogue?
  c. Why does every synagogue contain a reminder of the Ten Commandments?

2 Imagine you have a friend who has never been inside a synagogue. Write them a letter or an e-mail explaining what the inside of the building is like.

3 There are many objects in a synagogue which are special to Jews. Think of something that is special to you and try to explain what makes it special.

Extra activity

Some Jews say that the ner tamid symbolises the belief that the light of the Torah will shine for ever. Look up Psalm 119.5 and explain what you think this means.

Mosques

Muslims believe that anyone who helps build a mosque wins great favour with Allah. As the Prophet Muhammad said: 'He who builds a mosque for Allah's sake, Allah will build for him a house in paradise.'

A house of prayer

Each mosque is based on the first mosque built by Muhammad in Madinah. At one end of the building there is a courtyard where Muslims wash themselves thoroughly in running water before praying.

A Each mosque contains a minbar from where the imam delivers his sermon during Friday prayers

As they enter the prayer room, Muslims leave their shoes at the door. This is a sign of respect for Allah. There are no seats or cushions inside (picture B). The room is carpeted but there are no images or pictures on the walls. This is because the Qur'an forbids any representations of men or animals to prevent idol worship. However, geometric designs are allowed and some mosques are decorated beautifully with colours and patterns.

One wall of the mosque is marked with a niche to indicate the direction of the holy city of Makkah (**qiblah**). The niche is called the mihrab. Everyone faces the mihrab when they pray. The mihrab is said to symbolise the ear of God bending down to hear the prayers of all faithful Muslims. Many worshippers bring their own prayer mats with them when they come to pray. The design of these mats includes an arch, which is laid out on the floor to face the mihrab.

At one end of the prayer room there are portable steps leading up to a platform – the minbar (picture A). The **imam** sits on the platform to deliver his sermon during Friday prayers. He often leads the prayers in the mosque, the **salah**, although any male Muslim can do this. The imam is elected by the Muslim community. He is a learned and well-respected man who knows the teachings of the Qur'an and offers his advice and support to the Muslim community. He and his family are also expected to live pleasing lives to Allah.

There is also a row of clocks in many mosques. One of these shows the present time, while the other five indicate the times at which prayers are held each day.

Many mosques are community centres as well as places of worship. A youth club, a kitchen and a reading room for adults are likely to be on the premises. There will also be a school, called a **madrasah**, where children go after their ordinary school day to learn Arabic and study the Qur'an.

B Mosques are often simple buildings with little decoration so that nothing can distract worshippers from their prayers

The adhan

The **adhan** is the call to prayer. It is broadcast in or from the mosque five times a day in Arabic.
God is the greatest. God is the greatest. God is the greatest. God is the greatest. I bear witness that there is no God but Allah. I bear witness that there is no God but Allah. I bear witness that Muhammad is the messenger of Allah. I bear witness that Muhammad is the messenger of Allah. Come to prayer. Come to prayer. Come to security. Come to security. God is the most great. God is the most great. There is no God but Allah.

In the glossary

Adhan	Madrasah	Salah
Imam	Qiblah	

Find the answers

- Why are there no pictures or statues in a mosque?
- What is an imam?
- What is the mihrab?

Learning about, learning from

1 Write a sentence about each of the following to describe their purpose.
   a. A mosque.   **c.** The minbar.
   b. The qiblah.   **d.** The mihrab.

2 Read the adhan in the box.
   a. Which phrase is repeated more than any other? What do you think this is intended to teach?
   b. What do you think the words 'come to security' mean?

3 The Qur'an says that as God knows everything in heaven and earth so three men cannot come together in secret as Allah is always there with them. What lesson do you think the Qur'an is trying to teach?

Extra activity

The Prophet Muhammad said: 'Wherever the hour of prayer overtakes you, you shall perform it. That place is a mosque.' He was telling his companions something important about prayer and about mosques. What do you think it was?

Gurdwaras (1)

Sikh places of worship are called gurdwaras. The word 'gurdwara' means 'the doorway to the Guru'. Sikhs believe that any building becomes a gurdwara when it contains a copy of their holy book, the Guru Granth Sahib. Without the holy book no building can be a gurdwara. The teachings of the Gurus, which are found in the holy book, are read and studied in the gurdwara. Few Sikhs have a copy of the Guru Granth Sahib in their own homes because the holy book needs to have a room of its own.

God's house

A gurdwara can be identified by the flag – the nishan sahib – flying outside (picture A). The flag plays an important part in some Sikh festivals. Many gurdwaras also carry the inscription 'ik oankar' ('God is one') on the outside of the building to express the central belief of Sikhism – that there is only one God.

A notice just inside the door informs everyone that they must do the following three things before they enter the hall of worship:

- Take off their shoes.
- Cover their heads (men should wear turbans and women silk scarves).
- Empty their pockets of any cigarettes and alcohol.

Once people cross the threshold of a gurdwara they are treading on 'holy ground' and are expected to act with due respect.

The Guru Granth Sahib

There are no seats in the main room of the gurdwara. The worshippers sit cross-legged on a carpeted floor, the men on one side of the central aisle and the women on the other (picture B). There are two reasons for this:

- Everyone must sit beneath the Guru Granth Sahib. The holy book is placed on the takht at one end of the gurdwara. The Guru Granth Sahib must be present at every service held in the gurdwara to symbolise the presence of God. During acts of worship, worshippers take care that they do not turn their backs on the Guru Granth Sahib at any time as this would be disrespectful.
- Everyone sitting on the same level beneath the Guru Granth Sahib emphasises the Sikh belief that all people, men and women, are equal in the sight of God. It also shows that they accept the authority of the Guru Granth Sahib over them.

The scriptures are kept in a special room overnight and taken out carefully early in

A The flag flying outside this building is a public announcement that it is a gurdwara

the morning. The Guru Granth Sahib is always carried high above the heads of the people as it is put into place to show that no one is 'above' (more important than) the holy book.

Someone often stands behind the Guru Granth Sahib waving a **chauri**, a fan made of yak hair or nylon. The chauri is a symbol of authority because it was used in the past in the presence of royalty. The **granthi**, the official who is responsible for reading from the holy book, sits behind and slightly below it. However, during some services other people can carry out readings. When the Guru Granth Sahib is not being used it is covered in a silk cloth called a romalla.

In the glossary

Chauri   Granthi

 Find the answers

- What does the word 'gurdwara' mean?

- What must everyone do before entering a gurdwara?

- Why do Sikhs always place themselves 'below' the Guru Granth Sahib?

B Sikhs sit on the floor for a service in a gurdwara so that they are below, and under the authority of, the Guru Granth Sahib

 Learning about, learning from

1 Write one or two sentences about each of the following.
 a. The gurdwara.
 b. The Guru Granth Sahib.
 c. The nishan sahib.
 d. The granthi.

2 Sikhs believe that the gurdwara is a holy place where God can be found. Describe two ways in which they show this in their place of worship.

3 Do you think a book can be like a wise person – a guru? Are there any books which you might turn to for advice?

From the Guru Granth Sahib

Study of and meditation on the scriptures within the congregation is very important and Sikhs should visit the gurdwara as often as possible.

Extra activity

Sikhs are surrounded by many symbols of their faith in the gurdwara. Which ones do you think they might find the most powerful? Explain your answer.

Gurdwaras (2)

All services in the gurdwara are followed by a free meal – the langar – a custom which dates back to Guru Nanak. At that time in India various groups of Hindus were not allowed to mix or eat together. Guru Nanak was born a Hindu but he taught that these rules should be ignored because all people are equal in God's sight. The langar, which is also the name of the kitchen where the meal is served, came to symbolise this equality.

Later, when Guru Amar Das was the Sikh leader, those who came to consult him about religious matters were always treated to a meal before the talks began. At these meals, which involved everyone in the preparation and serving, all people were given exactly the same food and treated the same – emperors and servants alike. Sikhs have never forgotten this example and still follow it today.

The langar

While people are worshipping together, volunteers work in the langar to prepare the meal (picture A). The service is often relayed to them to encourage them to see that what they are doing is as an important part of worship. After the service, everyone – Sikh and non-Sikh alike – shares the meal. The food, which is always vegetarian so that no one need feel excluded, is made using only ingredients which are available in the Punjab. The food is blessed in the closing prayers of the service before the people stand or sit on the floor to eat together. Again, this is a reminder that everyone is equal in the sight of God.

Serving everyone

A gurdwara is never short of volunteers to provide the food, prepare and serve it (picture B). The work is seen as a **sewa**,

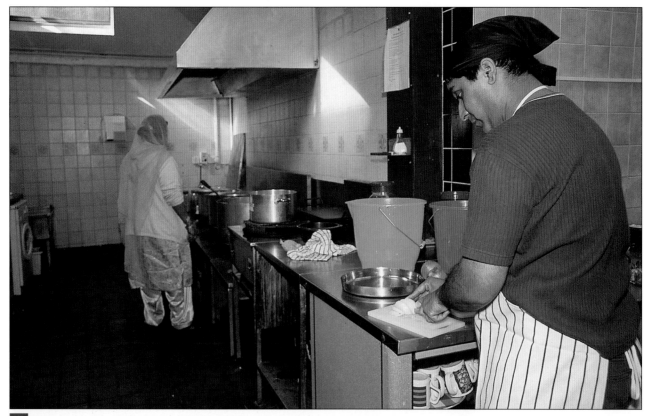

A Everyone in a gurdwara is expected to play their part in serving others by preparing the food to be served in the langar

an act of service to others. Often, if there is a happy family occasion such as the naming of a baby in the service, that family provides the food for everyone as a gift. Working together like this is a practical demonstration that no one is more important than anyone else in God's service. The need to serve others freely without any hope of reward is an important part of Sikh teaching.

It is important that the food is served to everyone present and not just members of the Sikh community. For their part, non-Sikh visitors are expected to share in the meal and they may offend their Sikh hosts if they decline. People who live close to the gurdwara are also invited to visit it regularly to enjoy a meal. Large Sikh temples are open every day of the week and serve thousands of meals to those in need.

B It is never too early to learn to serve others

By Guru Arjan

Let all share equally; no one should be seen as an outsider.

In the glossary

Sewa

Find the answers

- What are the two meanings of the word 'langar'?

- What draws together members of the Sikh community?

- How did Guru Nanak and Guru Amar Das lay the foundations for the langar?

Learning about, learning from

1 Why is the langar an important part of Sikh worship?

2 Read the quotation in the box. How do Sikhs put this into practice through their langar?

3 Write down five ways in which you could carry out the Sikh ideal of serving your local community. Do you think the principle of serving others without any thought of reward is an important one in today's world?

Extra activity

Many Sikh gurdwaras in Britain are old churches which are no longer used by Christians.

a. Describe the items you might need to take out of a church and what you would need to put into the building to convert it into a gurdwara.

b. How would everyone nearby know that the building had changed from a church into a gurdwara?

Mandirs

Hindu mandirs come in all shapes and sizes. In Britain, where there are thousands of Hindus, a house or a disused church may be converted into a mandir but there are also some buildings which have been specially designed and built for this purpose. For example, a magnificent mandir – the largest outside India – was opened in North London in 1995 to serve the needs of the Hindu community in the area. Hindus are not obliged to worship in a mandir and many rarely visit one. On the other hand, some Hindus go every week to place offerings at the feet of one of the statues of the gods or goddesses (**murtis**) (picture A).

Inside a mandir

Inside many mandirs there is a special room – called garbagriha – to which the smaller statues of the gods and goddesses are taken at night. In this special area they are washed and prepared for worship first thing in the morning by the priest. For larger statues a curtain is drawn around them before washing takes place. As part of this preparation the priest lays offerings of fruit, flowers and incense in front of the statues. On special festival days the statues are dressed in fine clothes and have a golden crown placed on their heads.

The main worship area is open to everyone. As they enter this area, worshippers must remove their shoes as a mark of respect because they are entering 'holy ground'. Like mosques and gurdwaras, mandirs have no seats and the worshippers sit together on the floor. Men, women and children sit and worship together in a mandir.

Special places and gods

Mandirs in India are usually built at places where a god has appeared at some

A Nearly all Hindu mandirs in Britain have been converted from houses or churches

time or is believed to have lived on earth. The special appearance of a god on earth is called an **avatar**. **Krisha** is one of the favourite Hindu gods and he is believed to have visited earth as an avatar nine times. Hindus are expecting him to appear one last time. Many mandirs are dedicated to Krishna. Brahman is the Supreme God and Krishna is one of the forms in which Brahman makes himself known.

Mandirs in India tend to be dedicated to the worship of one god. In Britain, however, most are dedicated to several gods and statues of each of them are placed inside. It is not the size or the beauty of the temple which makes it important to Hindus. What matters is the attitude of the worshippers as they come to present their offerings before the gods. If they come humbly into the presence of God and offer the sacrifices from the heart, they can be sure they will be accepted by God.

B Hindus are not under any obligation to attend the mandir for worship but many choose to do so

In the glossary

Avatar   Murtis
Krishna

Find the answers

- What is the name of a Hindu place of worship?
- To which god are many Hindu temples dedicated?
- What happens to the statues of the gods at night-time?

Learning about, learning from

1 a. What is the Hindu name for the statues of the gods and goddesses?
  b. What is the name of the room where the statues are kept?
  c. What is an avatar?

2 Describe one difference between mandirs in India and those in Britain.

3 Hindus can worship at home without going to a mandir but many visit the temple regularly. They value the experience of worshipping with others.
  a. List five things which are more enjoyable when they are done in the company of others. Why are they less enjoyable when done in private?
  b. Does this help you to understand why many Hindus prefer to worship with others? Explain your answer.

Extra activity

Hinduism has always encouraged the use of statues and images in the worship of God. Many other religions warn against the dangers of doing this. Can you think of one advantage and one disadvantage of using such images?

Buddhist temples

Many Buddhists have an image of the Buddha in their home, standing in a small shrine or on a high shelf. This is used as a constant reminder of the Buddha's teaching. They often focus their mind on the image as they meditate or present their offerings of flowers, light and incense.

Buddhist temples

Although Buddhists do not have to meet together to meditate, they often do so. Buddhists remove their shoes before entering the prayer room. Many different images of the Buddha (**rupas**) may be found in the shrine room in the temple (picture A). This is because there are many ways of showing the Buddha's enlightenment and each of them has their own meaning.

Worshippers place their hands together and make an offering in front of the statue. There are three offerings that can be made:

- Flowers. Flowers wither and die. This reminds everyone that the same will happen to them. Nothing in this world lasts for ever.
- Light. A light burns brightly and banishes the darkness.
- Incense. The smell of incense is fragrant, which reminds worshippers of the teaching of the Buddha.

Buddhist monasteries

In many countries, Buddhist monks live in monasteries. Boys from the age of about 11 often spend some months away from their parents in a monastery. There they receive a special education from the monks. Parents pay regular visits to their children.

Gardens are an important part of many monasteries. Not only are they places of peace and quiet but the plants and shrubs are symbols to teach that nothing in life lasts for ever – they grow, die and grow again through their seeds. Buddhists believe the same happens to humans – they believe strongly in reincarnation. Many monasteries also contain a pipal tree, the type of tree under which the Buddha was sitting when he was enlightened.

Stupas

Many Buddhists worship at stupas (picture B). These are chambers or burial mounds built to house the bones, hair or clothing of the Buddha. When he died his body was cremated and the ashes were taken to eight different places. Stupas were then built around them. Another stupa was built over the place where the body was cremated and a tenth where the container which held his ashes was buried. Later, many other stupas were built to honour special Buddhists.

A The prayer room of a Buddhist temple always has a statue of the Buddha to concentrate the minds of those meditating on his teaching

B There are now many stupas and these have become places of pilgrimage for Buddhists

A Buddhist prayer

This prayer is often said when flowers are laid in front of the Buddha as an offering:

I make the offering to the Buddha with these flowers and through this merit may there be release. Even as these flowers must fade so my body goes to destruction.

In the glossary
Rupas

 Find the answers

- Why do some Buddhists have an image of the Buddha at home?
- Why are there many different images of the Buddha?
- Why may boys in some countries spend time living in their local Buddhist monasteries?

Learning about, learning from

1 Read the quotation in the box.
 a. Why are flowers a popular offering to place before the Buddha?
 b. What do flowers constantly remind worshippers of?

2 Light and incense are also offered before the statue of the Buddha. Can you think of two reasons why these are appropriate offerings?

3 Buddhists often touch their chest, mouth and forehead when making an offering. What do you think these actions symbolise?

Extra activity

Why are Buddhist rupas placed on a high shelf in the home? Compare this with how Muslims treat the Qur'an and Sikhs the Guru Granth Sahib. What can you learn from these actions about the way worshippers treat holy or spiritual objects?

5 People at prayer

Introduction

Praying is an important religious activity. Many people pray regularly. Even those who are not sure whether or not they believe in God often pray in a crisis – when everything else has failed.

There are many possible reasons why people pray:

- *To talk to God*. We know that people often pray when they come together to worship in a holy place. Praying together is a part of most religions but it is not the only time when people pray. They often speak to God when they are on their own or with other members of their family. Parents and children, for example, often pray together at home.
- *To thank God*. Many people want to thank God for the beauty of the world in which they live or for the many gifts they have been given. At other times they pray because they feel dependent on God. Religious people often feel there are evil powers at work in the world and they need to feel God's protection in keeping them safe.

- *To ask for the forgiveness of their sins*. People may pray because they feel unworthy of God's kindness and goodness. This is a strong religious feeling. Sikhs, Muslims and Hindus partly express this feeling by washing themselves and removing their shoes before they pray. They are showing that prayer means something special to them. By washing they are trying to cleanse themselves from their sins.
- *To pray for others*. People often pray because they need to ask God to do something special for other people. Prayers said for other people are called intercessions. In all religious faiths, praying for others in need is very important.

For most people, praying involves using words. There is, however, a form of praying in which the worshipper is largely silent. This is called meditation. It involves a deep kind of reflection. In Buddhism meditation involves correct posture, a control of breathing and the concentration of one's thoughts. Followers of other religions also sometimes use meditation.

In this unit

In this unit you will read about the following:

- In their prayers, Christians follow the example of Jesus and use the prayer that he taught his disciples – the **Lord's Prayer**. Prayer plays an important part in Christian public worship. Some Christians pray to the Virgin Mary.

- For Jews prayer is important in the home and in the synagogue. Jewish men wear special clothes when they are praying. Special prayers and a family meal take place on the Sabbath Day.

- The most important Muslim prayers are those said around midday on Fridays in the mosque. For these each worshipper first performs a washing ritual – **wudu**. All Muslims perform their prayers facing the holy city of Makkah.

- The most important Hindu prayers are those said each morning in front of the shrine at home. Some worshippers also pray in the mandir.

- For Sikhs one prayer is more important than any other – the Japji Sahib, which is recited each day. The **Ardas** prayer is used in many public services of worship.

- Buddhists believe that meditation is an important spiritual exercise because it brings people to a deeper understanding of the meaning of life.

In the glossary

Ardas   Wudu
Lord's Prayer

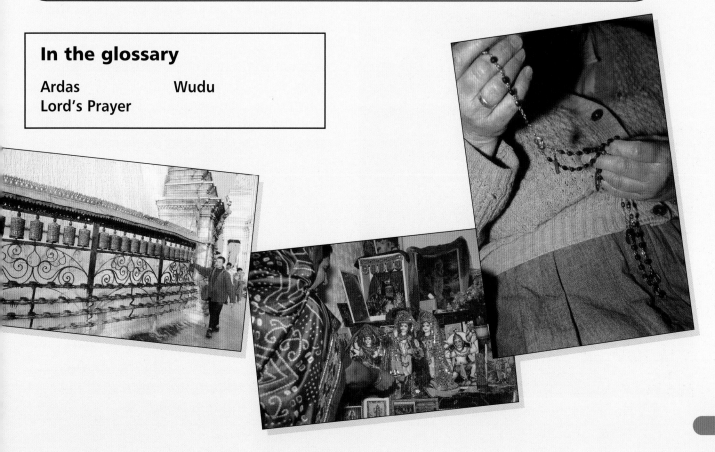

Christian prayer

Christians try to follow the example and teachings of Jesus. The Gospels say that Jesus often prayed to God, his Father. On several occasions, day and night, he went out alone to pray to God. Jesus prayed in particular before the important decisions and moments of his life. For example, he prayed before choosing his 12 disciples and before his arrest in the Garden of Gethsemane. Jesus made up a special prayer which he passed on to his disciples (see the box). This has been called the Lord's Prayer. The Lord's Prayer is still used by many Christians throughout the world today in acts of public worship.

A Praying is the most important spiritual activity in Christianity

Christians and prayer

Christians pray in many different ways. Children, for example, are often taught by their parents to kneel by their bedside to say prayers. Christian families sometimes pray together and read the Bible at the meal table.

Prayers form an important part of all Christian services. However, ways of praying in church differ (picture A). In Roman Catholic and Anglican services the prayers are usually taken from a prayer book. In Nonconformist churches the minister leads the congregation in unwritten prayers.

The Rosary and meditation

Some Roman Catholics use a **rosary** to help them in their personal prayers (picture B). This string of beads helps them to reflect on the life, death and resurrection of Jesus as they pray. While holding a rosary the worshipper repeats such prayers as the **Hail Mary**.

Roman Catholics often address their prayers to Mary, the mother of Jesus. Many Christians also meditate. This goes beyond praying with words, as believers allow their thoughts about God to really sink in.

The Lord's Prayer

This is the prayer that Jesus taught his followers to use:
Our Father in heaven, hallowed be your name, your kingdom come, your will be done on earth as it is in heaven. Give us our daily bread. Forgive us our debts, as we have also forgiven our debtors. And lead us not into temptation, but deliver us from the evil one.'

B This Roman Catholic nun is using a rosary

C This candle helps Christians to remember the needs of others as they pray

In the glossary

Hail Mary   Rosary

Find the answers

- Why is the Lord's Prayer the most important Christian prayer?
- How do some Christians try to make prayer a part of family life?
- What is meditation?

Learning about, learning from

1 **a.** When did Jesus often pray?
   b. Which prayer did Jesus teach his disciples to use?

2 What is the main difference between prayers in Roman Catholic and Anglican churches and those in Nonconformist churches?

3 What do you think a Christian may understand or feel about prayers that go unanswered?

4 Using books from the library and/or the internet, find out more about each of the following.
   a. The rosary.
   b. Meditation.
   Why do many Christians use them in their prayers?

Extra activity

Roman Catholics often pray to Mary because they feel unworthy to enter the presence of God directly. Do you think they are right to feel like this? Explain your answer.

Jewish prayer

Jewish synagogues hold three prayer services each day:

- In the morning, because Abraham prayed early in the day so that he could meet with God before the business of the day began.
- In the afternoon, because Isaac stopped what he was doing to pray to God in the afternoon.
- In the evening, because Jacob prayed to God in the evening to thank Him for the blessings of the day.

By praying three times a day Jews are following the example set by their ancestors. In practice, most Jews are unable to go to the synagogue for these prayers and so they pray at home. On each weekday morning a Jewish man puts on his **tefillin** – leather boxes which contain passages from the Torah. He winds one around his forehead to show that he is thinking about God, and one around his left arm, close to his heart, to show that he loves God. He places a yarmulke (a small skull-cap) on his head and a **tallit** around his shoulders (picture A). As well as obeying the scriptures in

A For Jews praying is the most important spiritual activity they perform

wearing the tefillin and tallit, they also make him feel special as he enters into God's presence.

The Sabbath Day

The Sabbath Day begins in the home at sunset on Friday evening, when the mother of the family lights the special candles and says a prayer from the prayer book, the Siddur:

> Blessed are you, O Lord our God, ruler of the universe who makes us holy by doing your commands and has commanded us to light the Sabbath candle.

The father says the kiddush. This traditional prayer, usually sung over a glass of wine, is an expression of happiness and joy. It includes the blessing:

> Blessed art thou, O Lord our God, King of the universe, who creates the fruit of the vine.

Two specially plaited loaves, called challah, sit on the table and these are blessed after the washing of hands, an action performed before bread is eaten in a Jewish home. At the same time, God is thanked for providing everything for people to enjoy:

> Blessed art thou, O God, King of the universe, who brings forth bread out of the earth.

It is said that in Judaism there is a prayer of thankfulness for absolutely everything because everything is a gift from God.

The Havdalah

The same note of thankfulness continues to the end of the Sabbath Day. The day ends at sunset on Saturday with more prayers of gratefulness. The **Havdalah** ('separation') service sees a plaited candle lit to symbolise a return to work after a day of rest and a spice box is passed around the family so that everyone can smell its fragrance. The prayer that ends the Sabbath Day hopes that the fragrance of the past hours will last through the week ahead.

B Almost all the prayers that a Jew is likely to use are found in the Siddur, the Jewish prayer book

A prayer from the Siddur

This prayer is said by every Jewish man when entering a synagogue:
And I, due to your great kindness, will come into your house and, in awe of you, I will worship facing towards your holy Temple... Lord, I love the dwelling of your house and the place where your glory rests. And I will worship and bow and bend my knee before God my maker. And, as for me, may my prayer come to you in an acceptable time; God, in your great kindness, answer me with the truth of your salvation.

In the glossary

Havdalah   Tefillin
Tallit

Find the answers

- What does a Jewish man wear when he prays?

- What is the kiddush and when it is said?

- What is the Havdalah and when does it takes place?

Learning about, learning from

1 Why do Jews pray three times a day?

2 Read the prayer in the box.
   a. What does this prayer say about God?
   b. How does this prayer give Jews the confidence to pray?

3 In one sentence, sum up the mood of a Jewish family as they eat the meal on Sabbath eve.

Extra activity

Some Jewish rabbis taught that the home is the true Temple, the parents are the priests and the kitchen table is the Ark. What were they trying to teach about prayer when they said this?

Muslim prayer

Prayer is at the heart of Islam. It is believed to be the only possible way to worship Allah. It is through prayer that each Muslim can be washed clean of their sins and receive guidance from Allah. Muhammad said that 'prayer is the essence of worship.'

Wudu

Muslims should pray five times day. Before praying they must wash themselves thoroughly (picture B). The special washing sequence is called wudu. The hands, mouth and throat, nose and face, arms up to the elbows, head, ears, and feet are all washed carefully more than once. Only when this sequence has been completed does a Muslim feel ready to enter into the presence of Allah.

Salah

Salah is a sequence of prayers which is performed with both words and actions. Each sequence is called a **rak'ah** (picture A). Two rak'ahs are compulsory during morning prayers, four at noon and in the afternoon, three at sunset and four at night. Preferably the rak'ahs should be performed in a mosque but they can be carried out in any clean place. During each rak'ah the worshipper stands, bows, kneels and touches the ground with his or her forehead. As he or she does so, words from the Qur'an are repeated.

Friday prayers

The most important prayers of the week are those held in the mosque on Friday mornings. Every male Muslim makes a great effort to be there. The imam leads all the worshippers through the rak'ah sequence. These prayers are always said in Arabic. As they pray, everyone faces towards the mihrab so that they are facing the holy city of Makkah (see the box on the next page).

Du'a

Muslims can say their own private prayers at any time and in their own language. These prayers, which are called **du'a**, are 'the prayers of the heart' and end with the worshipper brushing his hand across his face to show that he has received God's blessing.

Prayers in which a Muslim joins with others are the most important. Muslims are encouraged, however, to pray on their own. All that is needed for private prayers is a clean place. As this cannot be guaranteed, some Muslims use a prayer mat called a musulla. The mat should be placed facing towards Makkah, which is located using a small compass.

A In Islam men and women are not allowed to pray together, and it is usually only men who go to the mosque to pray

B No one is allowed to enter the presence of Allah to pray unless he has washed himself thoroughly first

Prayers in Makkah and Madinah

These words are by the Prophet Muhammad:

The prayer said in Madinah is worth thousands of others, except that in Makkah, which is worth a hundred thousand. But worth more than all this is the prayer which is said in the house where no one sees but God and which has no other object than to draw close to God.

In the glossary

Du'a   Rak'ah

 Find the answers

- What is salah?
- What is a rak'ah?
- Why might a Muslim use a prayer mat?

Learning about, learning from

1 **a.** What is wudu?
   b. How is wudu carried out?
   c. Why is wudu performed?

2 **a.** What are du'a?
   b. How are du'a different from salah?

3 The Qur'an says: 'Prayer restrains from shameful and unjust deeds.'
   a. Suggest why prayer may have a positive effect on the way some people behave.
   b. Do you think prayer would have this effect on you?

4 What do Friday prayers mean to every male Muslim?

 Extra activity

'A person's prayer mat is his mosque.' What does this quotation tell you about Muslim prayer?

Hindu prayer

Hindus can worship and pray either at home or in the mandir. However, it is the home which is at the heart of Hindu worship (picture A). Each Hindu home has a shrine, a place set apart for worship. Many Hindus rarely, if ever, go the mandir to offer their prayers and worship.

Prayer at home

A place in every Hindu home is set aside for worship. This could be a separate room, an alcove or a high shelf – anywhere is suitable. A statue or picture of the god or goddess who the family worships is placed there so that everyone can take part in prayers, from the youngest family member to the oldest.

The mother usually arranges the various acts of puja, or worship, for her family. She rises early, washes and puts on clean clothes before lighting the incense sticks or candles as well as setting offerings of food before the god. These offerings are not food for the god or goddess to eat. They are a way for the family to express that all good things in life come from **Brahma**, the Creator God. Making offerings is a way for people to show how grateful they are. These offerings form an important part of Hindu worship.

Prayer in the mandir

Prayer in Hinduism remains a personal thing even if it is offered with others in the mandir. The main difference between praying in the mandir (picture B) and praying at home is that prayers in the temple are led by a priest.

Hindus do not see prayer as a conversation between themselves and God. It is an opportunity to repeat God's name over and over again using different mantras. There are thousands of mantras. Hindus, however, usually repeat just one mantra throughout their lives. The one chosen will have often been suggested to them by their guru (spiritual advisor).

There are two reasons for repeating a mantra. Hindus believe that God himself is nameless even though he has been given thousands of different names. It is the repetition of one name which is most important. However, as the story on the next page shows, there is another reason for using a mantra. The recitation of God's name provides a kind of protection for the worshipper even if it is not needed until some time later.

A It is the Hindu mother's responsibility to organise the home shrine and the acts of worship carried out by the family

An old story

The importance of repeating God's name is illustrated by an old Hindu story. A very wicked old man accidentally spoke the name of God in the last few hours of his life and was saved from eternal death. His son was called Naryana, which is one of the names of God. By calling out his son's name as he was dying, the man was forgiven even though he had lived a wicked life.

B Even though worshippers in the temple pray together, they are offering their own individual prayers to God

A Hindu prayer

Hindus offer a special prayer each morning. It ends with the words:
Peace be in the heavens; peace be on earth.
May the waters flow peacefully.
May the plants grow peacefully.
And may that peace come to us.
Aum. Peace. Peace. Peace.

In the glossary

Brahma

Find the answers

- What do all Hindu families have at home to remind them of their god or goddess?

- What is puja?

- How are mantras used by Hindus?

Learning about, learning from

1 Explain in a sentence or two the meaning of the following words.
   a. Mantra.
   b. Guru.

2 Use picture A to help you write a paragraph to describe a shrine that a Hindu family might have in their house.

3 Much has been written in the Hindu holy books about the peace and beauty of the world around us. Temples in India are often built to resemble a mountain, with carvings of the gods at the top. How would you represent peace and beauty in a symbol or design?

Extra activity

The Bhagavad Gita, the most important scripture for most Hindus, says: 'A person may offer me [God] even a leaf, a flower, a fruit or a drop of water. When it is offered with love I will accept it.' Does it seem strange to you that the God who created everything should be offered a leaf, a fruit or a drop of water? Perhaps these are the most beautiful offerings of all? Explain your answer.

Sikh prayer

Prayer plays an important part in the everyday life of many Sikhs. They are encouraged to rise early in the morning to pray. After taking a bath they think deeply (meditate) on the name of God. As the Guru Granth Sahib tells them: 'After taking a bath, meditate on your Lord, and your mind and body will become pure.'

Sikhs also pray during the evening and last thing at night. On each occasion they use the set prayers known as nit nem, for which they learn the language of gurmukhi.

The Japji Sahib

Most Sikhs know all 38 verses of the Japji Sahib by heart. This is the long prayer with which the Guru Granth Sahib begins. They often recite the verses to themselves as they get ready for work in the morning or as they travel. Those who do not know this prayer can read it from the Gutka, a summary of the Guru Granth Sahib. The Japji Sahib, written by Guru Nanak himself, begins with the words: 'This Being is one, he is eternal.'

A Although praying is an important activity for Sikhs when they meet together, prayers are also performed in private

The Japji Sahib goes on to explain that everything in the universe has been created by God and is under his complete control. By reciting it all Sikhs are reminding themselves that there is one God, that he is all-powerful and that he should be worshipped. This is the basic teaching of Sikhism.

The Ardas

During morning prayers Sikhs also recite the Ardas (see the box on the next page). This important Sikh prayer is a reminder to all worshippers of the lives of the Gurus and others who have fought for the faith. It calls on God to help and forgive all Sikhs. The Ardas prayer is also recited in the gurdwara whenever a baby is dedicated or someone is initiated into the **Khalsa**. The prayer is also recited during a Sikh cremation.

Mala

Older Sikhs often use a mala to help them pray. This is a string of 108 beads which they pass through their fingers to prompt their prayers. With each bead they say 'Waheguru, Waheguru', which means 'Wonderful Lord, Wonderful Lord'. Some older malas are made of wool, with knots instead of beads.

The Guru Granth Sahib

Reading passages from the Guru Granth Sahib forms an everyday, but important, part of praying for a Sikh. This is particularly true when a family has gone through a difficult time such as bereavement or if they are faced with making a difficult decision. At these times the whole of the Guru Granth Sahib is read through in a spirit of prayer. This reading, called the **Akhand Path**, takes about 48 hours and involves many people from the Sikh community.

B There is a strong link between readings taken from the holy book, the Guru Granth Sahib, and praying in all Sikh worship

The Ardas

This is an extract from the Ardas prayer:

May Sikhism find a loving place in our hearts and serve to draw our souls towards thee. Save us, O Father, from lust, wrath, greed, undue attachment and pride... Grant the gift of faith, the gift of confidence in Thee... Grant that we may according to thy will do what is right. Give us light, give us understanding... Forgive our sins... Help us in keeping ourselves pure... Through Nanak may Thy Name forever be on the increase.

In the glossary

Akhand Path   Khalsa

Find the answers

- What does the Guru Granth Sahib say about prayer?

- What are the Japji Sahib and the Ardas?

- How do some Sikhs use a mala to help them pray?

Learning about, learning from

1 a. At which times in the day is a Sikh encouraged to pray?
   b. What must a Sikh do before he or she prays?

2 Explain in your own words the important part that prayer plays in the everyday lives of Sikhs.

3 Read the extract from the Ardas prayer in the box. It mentions several sins from which only God can save the worshipper.
   a. Using a dictionary if necessary, explain briefly what each of these 'sins' are.
   b. Greed and pride are things that Sikhs pray to resist. Write down an example of what greed and pride might mean in the modern world. Do you agree that they are bad things?

Extra activity

Write down three reasons why the early morning might be the best time for a worshipper to meet with God. Do you think it is a good time for people to pray?

Buddhist meditation

All Buddhists honour the Buddha. He not only discovered the path to enlightenment, he also dedicated himself to sharing that path with others. When they enter the shrine room in the temple, worshippers are inspired by the face of the Buddha's statue (picture A). In it they see the love and joy of the Buddha himself. These are the qualities they strive for in themselves.

Buddhists do not believe in one God or many gods, so prayer cannot be a two-way conversation. They cannot look to a power outside themselves for help, strength or guidance. Instead, meditation is a way of controlling their inner thoughts and feelings. By controlling them they also hope to control the suffering that these thoughts bring.

Beads and prayer wheels

Buddhists in Tibet have different religious practices from those in other countries. To help them pray they hold a string of beads called a mala, which can have 27, 54 or 108 beads. These beads can be made of seeds, wood or plastic and have two main uses:

- To help people keep count of the number of prostrations (bowings) or prayers that have been said.
- To concentrate thoughts during the different meditations. As they hold each bead, a mantra is chanted or the name of the Buddha is said. The circle of beads is a reminder of the main teachings of the Buddha. Tibetan Buddhists believe that the chanting of mantras is very important. Repeated often enough, they open up the mind to receive the truth.

In Tibet **prayer wheels** are a common sight in temples and monasteries (picture B). Mantras are inscribed on bronze cylinders which people spin around. The sounds and vibrations of the prayer wheels can be felt in all directions. Sometimes the prayer wheels are driven by electric or water power.

Mandalas

In most countries where many Buddhists live the temples are usually kept open. In Sri Lanka and Thailand, for example, Buddhists try to spend some time each day in religious activity. Through such activity, however simple it may be, the mind becomes both focused and calm. A popular activity for monks in these countries, as in India, is to make **mandalas** out of coloured sand. These are patterns of images with a spiritual meaning. Great care is taken over the smallest detail even though the mandalas are not kept when they are finished. Buddhists believe that a person should take great pride in everything they do, but also to learn to let them go.

A Buddhists find the inspiration for their meditation in the face of the Buddha

B Prayer wheels in Tibet encourage Buddhists in their faith

By the Buddha

The Buddha taught his followers:
The one who protects his mind from greed, anger and foolishness is the one who enjoys real and lasting peace.

In the glossary

Mandalas   Prayer wheels

 Find the answers

- What is a mala?

- What are prayer wheels used for?

- What is a mandala?

Learning about, learning from

1 a. Why are Buddhists inspired by statues of the Buddha?
   b. Why is Buddhist meditation different from prayer?
   c. What do Buddhists hope to achieve by meditating?

2 If you were given the opportunity to question a Buddhist about meditation, which questions would you ask? Write down a list of five questions.

3 Buddhists meditate to establish contact with their inner feelings. Do you have such feelings? If so, how do you contact them?

Extra activity

The quotation in the box says that the way to lasting peace is to control the mind from greed, anger and foolishness. How easy is it to control feelings like anger and greed? Would it be possible for you to stop yourself feeling these things? Explain your answer.

6 Religious festivals

Introduction

There are hundreds of religious festivals around the world each year. These festivals are usually linked to important people and events. For example, people may be celebrating:

- *the birth of a founder or leader*. At **Christmas** Christians celebrate the birth of Jesus, while Sikhs hold special festivals throughout the year, called **gurpurbs**, to mark the birth or death of a Guru.
- *the end of a fast or some other important religious occasion*. After the fasting and self-denial during the month of **Ramadan**, for example, Muslims look forward to the festival of **Id-ul-Fitr**.
- *a particularly important event in the history of their religion*. Each year, at Easter, Christians remember the death and resurrection of Jesus. Similarly, Jews recall the release of their ancestors from Egyptian slavery during the festival of Passover.
- *an important season of the year*. For example, many communities celebrate the gathering of the harvest because this is important to everyone. Although it now celebrates far more, the Jewish **Sukkoth** festival was originally held for this reason. The beginning of a new year is also a cause for celebration in many faiths.

Remembering the past and looking forward

Religious festivals are times for looking back to remember things past and looking forward with confidence and faith. They bring people together to recreate an event that is important to them. Symbols are used in festivals to help people reflect on, and understand, the past. Those celebrating the Passover, for example, are told to remember what happened 'as if you had been there' and the symbols used help them to do this.

Religious festivals have many features in common with each other. The giving and receiving of presents and cards is common to many such events, including Christmas and Id-ul-Fitr. So, too, is the preparation of special food and drink; the wearing of special or new clothes; the carrying of streamers; and the lighting of fireworks, firecrackers and bonfires. Singing, dancing, playing music and taking part in processions also play an important part in many religious festivals. Festivals can be light-hearted or serious, long or short, demanding or easy. In some religions, such as Christianity and Judaism, there are many festivals while in others, like Islam, there are just a few.

In this unit

In this unit you will read about the following:

- Christmas and **Advent** are Christian festivals looking forward to and celebrating the birth of Jesus. Light is a particularly important symbol in these festivals.

- **Lent** and **Holy Week** are long festivals preparing Christians to remember the death of Jesus. They are times of spiritual preparation.

- Easter is an important Christian festival when the death and resurrection of Jesus are celebrated.

- At **Pentecost** Christians remember the day on which the Holy Spirit was given and the Christian Church was born.

- **Rosh Hashanah** and **Yom Kippur** are the two most serious days in the Jewish year, allowing people time to seek God's forgiveness for their sins and to make a fresh start in their spiritual lives.

- At Passover Jews look back to the important event in their history when God led their ancestors out of slavery to the Promised Land of Israel.

- The Muslim festival of Id-ul-Fitr draws the fast of Ramadan to a close, while **Id-ul-Adha** is celebrated by pilgrims on the **Hajj** to Makkah and those remaining at home.

- The Hindu festival of **Divali** marks the beginning of a new year in business and in personal lives, while **Holi** is an important spring festival.

- Gurpurbs are Sikh festivals that mark a Guru's anniversary, while **melas**, such as **Baisakhi**, celebrate important events in Sikh history.

- There are several special Buddhist festivals that recall events in the Buddha's life. They also provide an opportunity for the monks to teach the people.

In the glossary

Advent	Id-ul-Fitr
Baisakhi	Lent
Christmas	Melas
Divali	Pentecost
Gurpurbs	Ramadan
Hajj	Rosh Hashanah
Holi	Sukkoth
Holy Week	Yom Kippur
Id-ul-Adha	

Advent and Christmas

The Christian year begins with Advent at the end of November or beginning of December. There are four Sundays in Advent, which lead up to the Christian festival of Christmas.

Advent

Advent is the time when Christians celebrate the coming of Jesus into the world as a baby. The birth of Jesus in the stable in Bethlemen is known to Christians as the Incarnation. During Advent Christians look forward to the 'coming' of Jesus and also to his 'Second Coming' to the earth at some time in the future.

Jesus was referred to by one of the Gospel writers as the 'light of the world', and many of the Advent celebrations are taken up with the contrast between light and darkness. On the four Sundays of Advent, special candles are lit in church and these are often set in an evergreen wreath or crown (picture A). Just as Jesus brought light into the world with his coming, so more candles are lit as Christmas approaches.

Christmas

While most Christian Churches celebrate Christmas Day on 25 December, some Churches keep the old date of 5 January. It is traditional for Christians to go to church for Midnight Mass on Christmas Eve, where the worship centres around the birth of Jesus, the Son of God. The Bible readings remind everyone of the events of the first Christmas and the importance of these events for Christians today.

There is often a crib in the church. The figure of the baby Jesus is not added to the crib until midnight on Christmas Eve (picture B). In many churches the main colours of the decorations are dark mauves and violets during Advent but these are replaced by white and gold at Christmas. These colours symbolise the purity (white) and kingship (gold) of Jesus.

A An Advent wreath reminds Christians of the buildup to the happy season of Christmas

Epiphany

The Christian festival of **Epiphany** follows 12 days after Christmas Day. This festival was once linked with the baptism of Jesus by John the Baptist in the River Jordan – it still is in the Orthodox Church. Now it is linked in some Churches with the visit of the Wise Men to the infant Jesus. They brought with them three gifts, which Christians see as symbolic:

- Gold for a king.
- Frankincense for a priest.
- Myrrh to show Christ's future suffering.

B Cribs are familiar sights in Christian churches as Christmas draws near

From the Nicene Creed

The Nicene Creed, a statement of Christian belief, probably dates from the fourth century CE:
We believe that... For us men and for our salvation he [Jesus] came down from heaven, by the power of the Holy Spirit he became incarnate [was born] of the Virgin Mary, and was made man.'

In the glossary
Epiphany

Find the answers
- Which symbols are associated with the festival of Advent?
- Which event is at the heart of the Christmas celebrations?
- Which two events in the Bible are linked with the festival of Epiphany?

Learning about, learning from
1 **a.** Which festival marks the beginning of the Christian year?
b. How long does this festival last?
c. Which two events associated with Jesus are Christians preparing themselves for at this time?

2 Describe in one sentence why each of the following festivals are important to Christians.
a. Advent.
b. Christmas.
c. Epiphany.

Extra activity
Many churches have a larger congregation on Christmas Eve than at any other time of the year. Do you think this means that Christmas is still a special spiritual time of year for many Christians or is it just tradition that takes them there?

Lent and Holy Week

Easter is an important Christian festival. It is the time when Christians remember the death and resurrection of Jesus. Easter begins in many churches with a time of preparation and reflection called Lent.

Lent

After he was baptised, Christians believe Jesus spent 40 days in the wilderness being tempted by the devil. Following the example of Jesus, many Christians spend the same length of time preparing themselves for the festival of Easter. This period of time is called Lent, which begins on Ash Wednesday. On this day in many churches crosses are burned from the previous Palm Sunday. The ash is used by the priest to mark the shape of a cross on the forehead of each worshipper (picture B). As the sign is made, the priest says: 'Remember, man, thou art but dust and to dust you shall return.'

During Lent many Christians try to follow the example of Jesus by resisting temptation. They do this by giving up something they enjoy, like eating chocolate. It is their way of trying to draw closer to God. Other Christians prefer to spend more time during this season praying and reading the Bible. There are extra services in most churches. Lent is a valuable time which strengthens a person's Christian faith.

Palm Sunday

Holy Week begins with Palm Sunday (picture A). This commemorates the beginning of the last week in the life of Jesus, when he entered the city of Jerusalem riding a donkey (see the box on the next page). In many Roman Catholic and Anglican churches palm leaves are blessed and scattered on the floor in front of the altar. In some churches worshippers process out of the building, often following a donkey, and walk around the local streets singing hymns.

A The entrance of Jesus into the city of Jerusalem on a donkey is celebrated by Christians on Palm Sunday

Maundy Thursday

Maundy Thursday follows four days after Palm Sunday. This day is important to Christians for two reasons:

- It was the day when Jesus took a towel and washed the feet of his disciples. He was showing them how God had called them to serve others. This tradition is kept alive in many Roman Catholic churches, with the priest washing the feet of 12 members of the congregation.

- It was the day when Jesus ate his last meal with his disciples. At this meal he gave them his 'greatest commandment' – that they should love one another. He also used the symbols of bread and wine to explain his coming death. This meal is relived by Christians every time they celebrate Holy Communion together, as they do on Maundy Thursday.

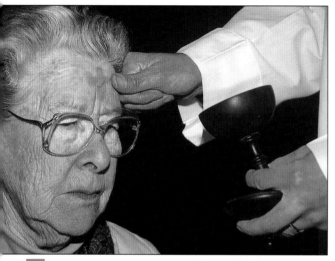

B The season of Lent begins on Ash Wednesday, when the mark of the cross is made on the forehead

Jesus enters Jerusalem

They brought the donkey and the colt, placed their coats on them, and Jesus sat on them. A very large crowd spread their cloaks on the road, whilst others cut branches from the trees and spread them on the road. The crowds that went ahead of him and those that followed began to shout: 'Hosanna to the Son of David! Blessed is he who comes in the name of the Lord! Hosanna in the highest.'

 Find the answers

- What is Lent?
- Which event do Christians remember on Palm Sunday?
- What is recalled by Christians on Maundy Thursday?

Learning about, learning from

1 a. Some Christians go to church to confess their sins before Lent begins. Why do you think they do this?

b. During Lent many Christians spend more time than usual praying. How might this help them to prepare for the festival of Easter?

2 a. Which event in the life of Jesus is remembered during Lent?

b. Why is this event important for Christians?

3 a. What was the 'greatest commandment' that Jesus gave to his disciples?

b. What was Jesus teaching everyone about the way to conduct their lives when he gave them this commandment?

 Extra activity

Why do many Christians feel that the events of the first Maundy Thursday were among the most important in the life and teaching of Jesus?

Easter

The Friday of Holy Week, **Good Friday**, is the most solemn day of the year for Christians. On this day the furnishings in many churches are removed or covered, leaving the building looking bare and empty (picture A). Worshippers often gather for three hours, from noon onwards, to 'watch' with Jesus as he faces the last few hours of his life.

Good Friday

The day is called 'Good' Friday because Christians believe their sins have been forgiven by the death of Jesus. As terrible as it was, the death of Jesus was necessary. Because Jesus died for our sins, Christians believe God is able to forgive those who are sorry for the sins they have committed. Special services are held in church, when descriptions of the death of Jesus from the Gospels are read. In some churches worshippers bow low before a cross and kiss it as a sign of respect. In Roman Catholic churches, worshippers visit the 14 Stations of the Cross – sculptures or pictures of events in the last few hours of the life of Jesus. They say a brief prayer before each Station (picture B).

Many churches come together on Good Friday to demonstrate their unity with each other. They may march through the streets behind a heavy wooden cross before joining together in a service. Sometimes Christians act out the death of Jesus, or they may erect crosses on a nearby hill so that everyone can see them and be reminded of the death of Jesus (picture C).

Easter Day

Easter Day is the most important day of the year for all Christians. On this day throughout the world they celebrate the rising of Jesus from the dead. The theme of the day is the 'new life' that Jesus offers to all through his own resurrection. Both Orthodox and Roman Catholic Christians begin their celebrations at midnight, when the darkness of the church gradually disappears as people light the candles they are holding. Members of the congregation symbolically 'search' for the body of Jesus in the church before announcing 'Christ is risen.'

The main Roman Catholic celebration is the Easter Vigil. A new fire is lit to represent the light of Christ and a large paschal candle – a tall candle which is specially

A The furniture is covered in some churches on Good Friday as a sign of mourning and respect

B This priest is standing in front of a Station of the Cross – worshippers travel around the Stations on Good Friday in the hours leading up to the death of Jesus

C Many churches see Good Friday as the best opportunity to share their faith with others

marked – is carried through the church to represent the coming resurrection. Readings are given from the **Old Testament** and the New Testament. A baby, an important sign of new life, is often baptised. An Easter **Eucharist** takes place.

The death of Jesus

Mark describes the death of Jesus: *They took Jesus to a place called Golgotha, which means 'the place of a skull'. There they tried to give him wine mixed with a drug called myrrh but Jesus would not drink it. Then they crucified him and divided his clothes among themselves, throwing dice to see who would get which piece of clothing. It was nine o'clock in the morning when they crucified him. At noon the whole country was covered with darkness. At three o'clock with a loud cry Jesus died.*

In the glossary

Easter Day	Good Friday
Eucharist	Old Testament

Find the answers

- What happens in many churches on Good Friday?
- What are the Stations of the Cross?
- What is the Easter Vigil?

Learning about, learning from

1 **a.** Which events in the life of Jesus are remembered by Christians on Good Friday?
   b. Which events in the life of Jesus are remembered by Christians on Easter Day?
   c. Why are both events so important to Christians?

2 Design an Easter poster or a wall hanging for a church illustrating Christian belief about the life, death and resurrection of Jesus.

3 **a.** Write down five things that would make a day perfect for you and explain your choices.
   b. Why are Christians particularly happy on Easter day?

Extra activity

The Christian belief about life after death is based on the resurrection of Jesus.
a. Why is the resurrection of Jesus important to Christians?
b Do you believe in life after death? Explain your answer.

Pentecost

The festival of Pentecost is celebrated 50 days after Easter and 11 days after some Churches celebrate Ascension Day. Ascension Day commemorates the time when Christians believe Jesus returned to his father in heaven (picture B). On this day some Churches hold a special Eucharist service when the paschal candle, lit for the first time on Easter Day, is finally put out. This reminds Christians that the risen Jesus is no longer with his followers on earth. Shortly, however, they will be celebrating the gift of the Holy Spirit (picture A).

The Day of Pentecost

Pentecost is the Jewish festival at which the disciples received the Holy Spirit (see the box on the next page). The Bible says that after Jesus left the earth his disciples gathered together in Jerusalem, afraid that the Romans would come to arrest them. As they did so a great wind blew through the room where they were gathered and God's Holy Spirit filled them. The Spirit gave them the power to speak to many people in their own language so that they could understand what was being said. Peter, the early Christian leader, summed up their message as:

> Repent and be baptised every one of you in the name of Jesus Christ for the remission of sins, and you shall receive the gift of the Holy Spirit.

Three thousand people were baptised on that day alone.

Celebrating Pentecost

Christians have always seen the first Pentecost as the birth of the Christian Church. It was on this day that the disciples began to preach the Christian message. In Britain this festival is often called Whitsun because it was a popular time in the past for baptising young Christians. During this service they wore white clothes, and 'White Sunday' became known as 'Whitsun'.

On Pentecost Sunday there are special services in church. During these services the priest talks about the work of the Holy Spirit in the Christian life. In some parts of Britain the day may also include a Whit Walk in which members of the congregation walk around the surrounding area singing hymns, reading passages from the Bible and preaching the Christian message.

A On the day of Pentecost the early Christians were given the gift of the Holy Spirit. The Holy Spirit is often depicted in the form of a dove.

B Forty days after he rose from the dead Jesus ascended to heaven – an event that some Christians celebrate on Ascension Day

The first day of Pentecost

When the day of Pentecost came, they were all together in one place. Suddenly a sound like the blowing of a violent wind came from heaven and filled the whole house where they were sitting. They saw what seemed to be tongues of fire that separated and came to rest on each of them. All of them were filled with the Holy Spirit and began to speak in other tongues, as the Spirit enabled them.

Find the answers

- Which event is celebrated by Christians at Pentecost?

- Why is this festival often called Whitsun?

- How do Christians today celebrate Pentecost?

Learning about, learning from

1 a. What do Christians believe happened between the resurrection of Jesus and the giving of the Holy Spirit at Pentecost?
  b. How do some Christians celebrate Ascension Day?

2 Use the description in the box and the text on these pages to help you write about what might have happened on the first day of Pentecost. Write a brief description in your exercise book or file. You will need to read Acts 2.1–13 for more information.

3 The word 'spirit' is not easy to understand.
  a. What do you think the word means?
  b. List two ways in which the word is used today.
  c. At Pentecost Christians speak of God as 'Spirit'. What do they mean by this?

Extra activity

Read the accounts given in Luke 24.36–53 and Acts 1.3–9 of the ascension of Jesus into heaven. Why do you think many Christians have difficulty understanding, and celebrating, this event?

Rosh Hashanah and Yom Kippur

There are many festivals in Judaism. Rosh Hashanah (New Year) and Yom Kippur (the Day of Atonement), held in early autumn, are the two holiest days in the Jewish year. These festivals provide an opportunity for everyone in the Jewish community to seek God's forgiveness and make a fresh beginning in their life.

Rosh Hashanah

Rosh Hashanah is a day of complete rest and marks the beginning of a time of self-examination for all Jews. On this day they wish each other well for the coming year by dipping a piece of apple into honey and eating it. They also break off pieces of bread, sprinkle them with sugar and say: 'May it be the Lord's will to renew us for a year which will be good and sweet.'

A On Rosh Hashanah God weighs the deeds of all Jews, as this stained-glass window reminds them

At Rosh Hashanah Jews remember two events:

- The creation of the world in six days by God and his resting on the seventh day.
- The judging of the Jewish people by God in heaven and the opening up of the Books of Life. It is believed that everyone's name is written in these books. God 'weighs up' the good and bad deeds committed by everyone in the past year before deciding whose name can remain there for the coming year (picture A).

In the synagogue the shofar, or ram's horn, is blown 100 times on Rosh Hashanah (picture B). The shofar makes three different sounds when it is blown and these are said to resemble the cries of the people before God as they realise how much they have sinned. The blowing of the shofar also encourages Jews to put right any wrongs they may have committed and to do better in the future.

Yom Kippur

Yom Kippur, the Jewish Day of Atonement, follows ten days after Rosh Hashanah. This 'day', lasting 25 hours, is one of fasting and is spent mainly in the synagogue. In a reading from the Torah worshippers are reminded of the example of Abraham, the father of the Jewish nation. He was willing to trust God, even when God told him to sacrifice his only son. The story of Jonah, the prophet, is also read from the scriptures. He did not want to obey God when told to preach to the wicked people of Nineveh. When he did so, however, the people repented of their sins and were forgiven. God will always forgive those who seek his forgiveness.

Jews believe that, on Yom Kippur, God decides whether a person's name should remain in the Books of Life or whether that person should die. It is also the day for remembering those in need in the world and those who have died for their faith. In particular, the six million Jews who were put to death by the Nazis during the Second World War are remembered.

B The blowing of the shofar is an important part of the festival of Rosh Hashanah

The first Rosh Hashanah

This extract comes from the Jewish scriptures:

The Lord said to Moses: 'Say to the Israelites: On the first day of the seventh month you are to have a day of rest, a sacred assembly commemorated with trumpet blasts. Do no regular work.'

Find the answers

- What do Jews celebrate at Rosh Hashanah?
- What is the shofar?
- How do Jews find inspiration from the life of Abraham on Yom Kippur?

Learning about, learning from

1 a. What is the Jewish New Year called?
b. What is the Jewish Day of Atonement called?

2 a. How many times is the shofar blown on Rosh Hashanah?
b. What do the sounds of the shofar represent?
c. Why is the blowing of the shofar appropriate for Rosh Hashanah?

3 At Rosh Hashanah people break off pieces of bread and wish each other a 'good and sweet' year ahead. What would make a good and sweet year for you?

Extra activity

Jews believe that on Yom Kippur God decides whose names will remain in the Books of Life.
a. What difference do you think this makes to the way that every Jew lives?
b. Do you think it would be a good idea to have a day when you think about your actions and try to put right any wrong things you may have done?

Passover

The festival of Passover, or Pesach, commemorates the most important event in Jewish history. The Jewish scriptures tell how, after more than 400 years of Egyptian slavery, the Jews were finally released and made their way to the land of Canaan (Israel). It took them 40 years to complete this journey, an event known to Jews as the Exodus. It is this journey which is remembered at Passover.

Preparing for Passover

Most of the Passover celebrations take place at home rather than in the synagogue. Weeks before the festival, the work of spring-cleaning the home begins. On the night before Passover starts, the children take part in a game of searching for any pieces of unleavened bread that have been hidden in the house. Behind the fun there is a serious message. The Jews had to leave Egypt in a hurry. They were so rushed there was no time for the bread dough that was already in the oven to rise. Therefore, the only bread they eat during Passover is matzah – unleavened loaves made without yeast.

The seder table

At the beginning of Passover a special family supper called seder ('order') is celebrated at home (picture A). During this meal a sequence of readings from the special service book, the Hagadah, tells the whole story of the journey out of Egypt. On the table are several foods, each in their own dish, which also help to tell the story (picture B). Two of these foods are symbolic and are not eaten:

- A roasted egg. This is a reminder of the festival sacrifice brought to the Temple in Jerusalem in ancient days.
- A roasted lamb bone. This represents the Passover lamb which used to be sacrificed in the Temple.

These foods are not eaten because the Temple was destroyed in 70 CE and animal sacrifices ended.

Four items on the table are eaten:

- Bitter herbs. These are a reminder of the bitter lives of those in Egyptian slavery.
- Green vegetables, usually parsley. These remind everyone that this is a spring festival.
- A mixture of chopped apple, nuts, cinnamon and wine, called haroset. This symbolises the cement used by the Israelites to build Egyptian houses when they were slaves.

A The family meal is at the heart of the Passover celebrations

- Salt water. This represents the tears of the Israelites during their long years of slavery.

As the story unfolds, the parsley is dipped in the salt water and the bitter herbs in the haroset to help everyone to experience the sorrow and bitterness of their ancestors' experience for themselves. In Egypt the Jews lost their freedom – they were in slavery. At Passover Jews pray for people who are still in slavery today.

B Each item on the seder plate is used as a reminder of the delivery of the Jews from Egyptian slavery

The four promises

Four promises were made by God to Moses. The seder service reminds everyone of them:
Say therefore to the people of Israel: 'I am the Lord and I will bring you out from under their bondage, and I will redeem you with an outstretched arm and with great acts of judgement. I will take you for my people and I will be your God.'

Find the answers

- What is remembered during the Passover festival?
- Which Jewish prayer book tells the story of Passover?
- What do Jews pray for at Passover?

Learning about, learning from

1 **a.** Which special foods are eaten at Passover?
   b. What do these foods represent?

2 **a.** What are Jewish children encouraged to do on the eve of Passover?
   b. What is the reason for this tradition?

3 Imagine you are a Jewish girl or boy. Explain why the night before the beginning of Passover is one that you look forward to very much.

Extra activity

Most of the celebrations of Passover take place in the home and not in the synagogue.
a. What do you think is the significance of this?
b. As a Jewish parent why would you feel it is important to pass on the traditions of Passover to your family, even if you no longer attended the synagogue?
c. What important things have learned from your parents and how have they passed them on to you?

Muslim festivals

There are two important festivals in Islam – Id-ul-Fitr and Id-ul-Adha. An Id ('happy festival') is a time when Muslim families come together, wear new clothes, give cards and presents to each other, donate money to charity and spend time in the mosque.

Id-ul-Fitr

Ramadan is the name of a month in the Islamic calendar and the time when Muslims fast during daylight hours. This fasting is an obligation for all healthy adult Muslims. After 30 days of fasting, Muslims celebrate the festival of Id-ul-Fitr, the festival of fast-breaking.

The fast of Ramadan ends with the rising of the new moon. This means that the date of the fast changes each year. For the feast of Id-ul-Fitr, shops in Muslim communities stay open late, homes are decorated, and presents and cards are exchanged. Everyone wears new clothes to attend special prayers in or around the mosque. The prayers are often held in the open air so that as many people as possible can attend. At the end of prayers, Muslims greet one another with the words 'Id Mubarak' ('have a happy festival').

Separate areas are provided for the men and women because they do not pray together. As was the practice of the Prophet Muhammad, Muslims travel from their home to the Id prayers by one route and return home by another. The spirit of the festival is one of love and the time is spent, after prayers, with members of the family. As the day finishes, many Muslims visit the graves of their relatives to say a special prayer for those who have died.

Id-ul-Adha

The Muslim festival of Id-ul-Adha takes place during the Hajj, the journey that millions of pilgrims take each year to the holy city of Makkah. When they reach the town of Mina on the Hajj the pilgrims sacrifice an animal, such as a sheep, goat, cow or camel. This reminds them of the willingness of Ibrahim (Abraham) to sacrifice his son as God had told him to do. By following in his footsteps, Muslims are showing a willingness to sacrifice everything for Allah.

Muslims at home celebrate Id-ul-Adha by wearing their best clothes and attending the mosque for special Id prayers. Those who can afford it are encouraged to buy a special Id sacrifice. After it has been cooked, a third of the meat is distributed to the poor. The remainder can be eaten at home or given away to relatives.

A During the Muslim festivals special time is set aside for reading and studying the Qur'an

B Children are introduced gradually to the demands that celebrating the festivals will make on them when they become adults

 **Find the answers**

- What is the link between Ramadan and Id-ul-Fitr?
- What happens during Id-ul-Adha?
- What does 'Id Mubarak' mean?

Learning about, learning from

1 **a.** What is fasting?
  b. What is Ramadan?
  c. How can a person know when to start and end their fast each day?

2 **a.** What is Id-ul-Fitr?
  b. When does Id-ul-Fitr start?
  c. What happens at Id-ul-Fitr?

3 **a.** Fasting plays an important part in several religions. Do you think you could benefit spiritually in any way from going without food for a short time?
  b. What do you think Muslims hope to gain from the experience?

Extra activity

Why is Id-ul-Fitr spent with other members of the family? How does visiting the graves of relatives fit in with this?

Starting Ramadan

The Qur'an lays down a simple rule for starting the fast of Ramadan each day:

Eat and drink until you can tell a white thread from a black one in the light of the coming dawn. Then resume the fast until nightfall.

Hindu festivals

Hinduism is a religion with many festivals, two of the most popular of which are Divali and Holi. These are celebrated by Hindus throughout the world.

Divali

In Hindu homes and businesses, the five-day festival of Divali marks the beginning of a new financial year. During Divali (also called the 'festival of lights'), houses, mandirs and other buildings are decorated with rows of lights. In the past the lights were placed in tiny clay holders called divas, which give the festival its

A The goddess Lakshmi plays an important part in the festival of Divali

name. Now, however, electric light bulbs are more likely to be used.

There are many stories and customs associated with Divali. In some parts of India it gives people the opportunity to welcome Lakshmi, the goddess of prosperity, into their homes – as long as the homes are clean and tidy (picture A). Therefore, the days before the festival begins are spent spring-cleaning. If Lakshmi visits, the family can look forward to good fortune in the coming months, both at home and in business.

Husbands and wives take this opportunity to renew their wedding vows to each other. Parents and children are reminded of the responsibilities they have to each other. All business account books are brought up to date and outstanding debts are cleared. Divali is a time for new beginnings. People buy new clothes and household equipment. Music and dancing goes on in the streets. Floats pass by, telling some of the traditional stories associated with the festival.

Holi

Holi is a spring festival which is celebrated by Hindus everywhere, although there are many different stories associated with this time. Holi takes its name from one such story in which the evil princess, Holika, tried to kill her nephew, Prahlada, because of his devotion to the god Vishnu. Prahlada was only saved from death because he repeated Vishnu's names. In the end it was Holika, and not Prahlada, who died in a bonfire. This story teaches Hindus about the importance of having faith and trust in God.

Many stories associated with the god Krishna are also linked with this festival. Krishna is one of the most popular Hindu

B People throw coloured dye over each other during Holi

gods who has visited the earth nine times. Part of Krishna's popularity comes from the practical jokes and tricks he played on the people he met. This spirit is recaptured at Holi as children throw coloured dye and water over people in the streets (picture B). In many villages in India the priest lights a huge bonfire and the men and boys dance around it.

Find the answers

- What important part does light play in the festival of Divali?

- Where does the name Holi come from?

- Who was Prahlada and how was he saved from death?

Learning about, learning from

1 What is the link between Lakshmi and the festival of Divali?

2 a. How do Hindus show that Divali is a festival for making a fresh start?

b. Do you think it is important to have a festival that allows people to make a fresh start in their lives? Explain your answer.

3 a. Why is Holi a time when Hindus play practical jokes on each other?

b. What do Hindus celebrate at Holi?

Extra activity

Lakshmi is an important goddess. As the goddess of prosperity and good fortune, every Hindu wants her to visit their home. Write a poem or a prayer that a Hindu might say to encourage Lakshmi to visit.

Sikh festivals

There are two kinds of religious festivals in Sikhism:

- Gurpurbs – festivals on which the birth or death of one of the Gurus is remembered.
- Melas – fairs. These often have the same name as Hindu festivals but the two religions have their own reasons for celebrating them.

Gurpurbs

Among the most important Sikh festivals are gurpurbs – holy days held to honour a Guru. The most important part of a gurpurb is the reading of the Guru Granth Sahib from beginning to end without a break. This reading, called the Arkhand Path, takes about 48 hours. It is timed to end on the morning of the festival, with all the readers being drawn from those members of the local Sikh community who can read garmukhi clearly and with understanding. Each reader must wash their hands immediately before touching the holy book and be ready to take over from the previous reader without a noticeable break.

The most important gurpurb is held to commemorate the birthday of Guru Nanak in 1469 CE. During this a procession is held, with five people dressed in yellow representing the **panj piares** – the first five members of the Khalsa. The Khalsa is the brotherhood of committed Sikhs. A gurpurb is also held to remember the birthday of Guru Gobind Singh, the founder of the Khalsa. The death of the fifth Guru, Arjan, is also commemorated because he was the first Sikh martyr.

Melas

Baisakhi is the most important Sikh mela, commemorating the birth of the Khalsa in 1699 CE (picture A). This is the favourite time for holding the **Amrit Sanskar** ceremony, when new members are initiated into the Khalsa. Services are held in the gurdwara and food is served in the langar all day. Special readings are given from the Guru Granth Sahib, together with poems to emphasise the importance of the occasion. During the Baisakhi celebrations the nishan sahib – the Sikh flag which flies outside every gurdwara – is taken down to allow the flag and flagpole to be washed (picture B). The yellow covers which are wrapped around the flagpole and the flag itself are replaced during this ceremony.

Both Sikhs and Hindus celebrate the festival of Divali, although for totally different reasons. At this festival Sikhs remember the sixth Guru, Har Gobind, who was released from prison – an event the people of Amritsar mark by lighting lamps in their houses. In 1680 CE the tenth Guru began the festival of Hola Mohalla at the same time as a Hindu festival to persuade the people to choose between the two religions.

A Processions, like this one at Baisakhi, are important ingredients of Sikh festivals

B During the festival of Baisakhi, the flag outside the gurdwara is washed and replaced

From the Guru Granth Sahib

He who thinks of no one but the true God... in whose heart the light of the Perfect One shines... Only he can be recognised as a pure member of the Khalsa.

In the glossary

Amrit Sanskar   Panj piares

 **Find the answers**

- What is the Akhand Path?

- What is the Khalsa and who founded it?

- What is the nishan sahib?

Learning about, learning from

1 a. What is a gurpurb?
   b. What is a mela?
   c. Give one example of a gurpurb and one example of a mela.

2 a. Why do Sikhs take so much care to ensure that the reading of the Guru Granth Sahib in the Akhand Path goes smoothly?
   b. Why do Sikhs wash and replace their flag each year?

3 Read the quotation in the box. What do you think it means when it speaks of the one 'in whose heart the light of the Perfect One shines'?

Extra activity

Many religions make heavy demands on their followers. Sikhism asks that they should be prepared to pay the ultimate price for their faith – that of life itself. Do you think anything could be so important that you would be prepared to give up everything for it – even your life? Explain your answer.

Special Buddhist days

Buddhist festivals bring people together to worship and to learn more about the teaching of the Buddha. However, the festivals themselves are not of particular importance. The Buddha himself taught that the only value of festivals lay in the attitude of mind that each worshipper brings to the celebration. Among the main Buddhist festivals are **Wesak**, Rainy Season Retreat and New Year.

Wesak

Wesak ('Buddha Day') is a Theravada (one of the two main schools of Buddhism) festival that celebrates the three main events in the Buddha's life – his birth, enlightenment and death. Buddhists send cards to each other decorated with symbols that remind people of the Buddha, such as the Wheel of Life, the Bodhi tree and the lotus flower. In some countries homes are decorated with candles during Wesak. The name of the festival comes from the month in which it is celebrated.

Rainy Season Retreat

At the time of the Buddha the wandering monks were criticised for walking through flooded fields during the rainy season and damaging the young rice shoots. Moving about during this time was, in any case, very difficult. The Buddha, therefore, told them to stay in the one place during this season. Although the situation has changed since then, many monks still gather for a retreat in the autumn.

During the Rainy Season Retreat Buddhists present the monks with the things they will need in the year ahead, such as material for new robes. The monks sew the cloth into robes by dawn the following day. Giving the monks what they need gives ordinary Buddhists the opportunity to build up some merit. Both the beginning and the end of the retreat are celebrated with festivals. It is the Kathina festival which draws the Rainy Season Retreat to a close.

New Year

Each Buddhist country has its own New Year festival. In Japan, bells in Buddhist temples are rung 108 times – once for each of the 'mortal passions' such as envy, malice or anger that distract people from taking the path to enlightenment. Buddhists believe each ringing of the bell drives out one of these passions.

Water is an important symbol of cleansing in many New Year celebrations. People wash the Buddha images and spray each other with water. Attempts are made to rescue any fish left stranded in dried-out streams and ponds. Birds are released from their cages.

Sometimes people make large images of the Buddha out of butter, which gradually melt and lose their shape and beauty. This

A Buddhist festivals bring people together to worship the Buddha

is done as a reminder that everything, even the most beautiful things, wither and die in the end. Great care is also taken over the making of mandalas out of sand. In this way Buddhists learn that it is important to create beautiful things, to love them and then to let them go.

B Monks making a mandala – a detailed pattern with a spiritual meaning – out of sand

In the glossary

Wesak

Find the answers

- What did the Buddha teach about the value of religious festivals?

- What is the Rainy Season Retreat?

- What do Buddhists hope to gain by giving gifts to the monks during the Rainy Season Retreat?

Learning about, learning from

1 **a.** Which three events in the life of the Buddha are celebrated on Wesak day?
  b. How do people decorate the cards they exchange on this day?
  c. Why is the festival called Wesak?

2 Buddhists often visit the graves of their loved ones at the end of a festival. Find out more about this activity using books from the library and/or the internet.

3 Buddhists often lavish great care in making mandalas out of sand. When they disintegrate it shows that we must learn to let everything in life go in the end.
  a. Do you think people can become too attached to things? Give an example of how this can cause problems to some people.
  b. Do you agree that it is important to learn to let all things go in the end?
  c. What things would you find most difficult to let go?

Extra activity

The Buddha taught that the only value of festivals lay in the spiritual attitudes they helped to foster. Write a paragraph to sum up what you think the main benefits of celebrating religious festivals might be.

Glossary

A

Abraham	The person considered by the Jews to be the father of the Jewish nation; received the promise from God that his descendants would inherit the land of Israel.
Absolution	The pronouncement by a priest that a person's sins have been forgiven; likely to happen in the Roman Catholic and some Anglican churches.
Adhan	The Muslim call to prayer, given from the minaret of the mosque.
Advent	The Church season that prepares people for the coming of Jesus at Christmas.
Agnostics	People who are not sure whether God exists or not.
Akhand Path	The unbroken reading of the Guru Granth Sahib in the gurdwara; usually carried out on some special occasion or when an important decision is to be made.
Allah	The name in Islam for God in the Arabic language.
Altar	The raised platform at the eastern end of most churches, from where worship is conducted.
Amrit	Holy water made from sugar and water; used by Sikhs in their initiation ceremonies such as the naming of a child or becoming a member of the faith.
Amritsar	The Sikh sacred city in the Punjab; home of the Golden Temple.
Amrit Sanskar	The Sikh ceremony at which members are initiated into the faith.
Anglican Church	Churches worldwide which follow the teachings of the Church of England and which accept the leadership of the Archbishop of Canterbury.
Ardas	The most important Sikh prayer; draws every act of worship in the gurdwara to a close.
Ark	The cabinet in the synagogue which houses the scrolls of the Torah; covered with a curtain when the scrolls are not in use.
Athiests	People who do not believe that God exists.
Avatar	The visit of a Hindu god to earth in the form of a human being or an animal.

B

Baisakhi	An important Sikh festival which celebrates the formation of the Khalsa in 1699 CE.
Bar mitzvah	'Son of the commandment'; a Jewish boy's coming of age at 13 years old, marked by a ceremony and family celebration.
Believer's baptism	The baptism of adults in the Baptist Church.
Bible	The Christian scriptures containing the Old and New Testaments; used by Christians in private and public worship.
Bishop	A senior priest who carries the responsibility for all the churches in an area, ordains priests and performs confirmations.
Blasphemy	Any thought or action which shows contempt for God.
Bodhisattva	A Buddhist who becomes enlightened and then remains on earth to help others to reach enlightenment.
Brahma	The Hindu Creator God.
Brahman	The Supreme God in Hinduism; the holy power which runs through the whole universe.
Buddha	Siddhartha Gotama, who became the Enlightened One; gave the teaching upon which Buddhism is based.

C

Cathedral	The main church in a diocese; contains the 'bishop's chair' from where the bishop conducts many of the services.
Chauri	The fan which is waved over the Guru Granth Sahib in a Sikh gurdwara; made of yak hair or nylon and a symbol of the authority of the scriptures.
Christmas	The Christian festival which is celebrated on 25 December; commemorates the birth of Jesus.
Church	The building where Christians meet for worship.
Church of England	The main Christian Church in Britain; also called the Anglican Church.
Circumcision	An operation carried out on male babies in both Judaism and Islam at eight days old; involves the removal of the foreskin of the boy's penis.

	Confession	A sacrament of the Catholic Church; a meeting at which a priest hears a person's confession of sins and grants them God's forgiveness.
	Crucifix	A cross containing the body of Jesus.
D	**Divali**	The Hindu festival of lights at the end of one year and the beginning of the new year.
	Du'a	Personal prayers in Islam; prayers which are voluntary and not compulsory.
	Dukkha	The first of the Four Noble Truths in Buddhism, which says that suffering is in the nature of human existence.
E	**Easter**	The Christian festival at which believers remember and celebrate the death and resurrection of Jesus.
	Easter Day	The day at the end of the festival of Easter when Christians celebrate the resurrection of Jesus.
	Epiphany	The Christian festival which celebrates the visit of the Wise Men to the infant Jesus; celebrated 12 days after Christmas.
	Eucharist	The 'act of thanksgiving'; the name given in many Churches to the service of Holy Communion when the death of Jesus is remembered.
	Exodus	The journey out of Egyptian slavery taken by the Jews to the country of Canaan (Israel).
F	**Five Ks**	The five symbols given to all who become members of the Sikh Khalsa.
	Font	A stone or wooden receptacle inside many churches; holds the water that is used in infant baptism.
	Four Noble Truths	The beliefs on which the teaching of Buddhism are based; deal with the existence of suffering and the answer to it.
G	**Golden Temple**	The most holy building in Sikhism; built in the middle of a sacred pool in Amritsar between 1577 and 1589 CE.
	Good Friday	The day in the Christian year after Maundy Thursday when Christians remember the death of Jesus on the cross.
	Gospels	Four books at the beginning of the New Testament in the Bible; each Gospel describes the life and teaching of Jesus.
	Granthi	An official in a gurdwara who reads the Guru Granth Sahib many times a day; officiates at Sikh services and ceremonies.
	Gurdwara	'The doorway to the Guru'; the Sikh place of worship.
	Gurpurbs	The anniversary of a Guru's birth or death, marked by the holding of a festival.
	Guru Granth Sahib	The Sikh scriptures, which were put together by Guru Arjan and completed by Guru Gobind Singh.
	Guru Nanak	The first Guru; the founder of the Sikh faith (1469–1539 CE).
	Gurus	Teachers; in Sikhism the title is used only for the ten human Gurus, for the Guru Granth Sahib and for God – the 'True Guru'.
H	**Hail Mary**	An important prayer addressed to the Virgin Mary; used in Roman Catholic churches.
	Hajj	The annual pilgrimage to Makkah and other holy places which all Muslims are expected to undertake at least once in their lives.
	Havdalah	The service which draws the Sabbath Day to a close in a Jewish family; 'separates' the Sabbath Day from the rest of the week.
	Hijrah	The journey of Muhammad and his followers from Makkah to Madinah in 622 CE; the Islamic calendar starts from this date.
	Holi	The Hindu spring festival dedicated in many parts of India to the god Krishna.
	Holy Communion	The service held in most Christian Churches to commemorate the death of Jesus; also called the Mass, Divine Liturgy, Eucharist and Lord's Supper.
	Holy Liturgy	The name given to the service of Holy Communion in the Orthodox Church.

	Holy Spirit	The third person in the Christian Trinity with God the Father and God the Son.
	Holy Week	The week in the Christian year that starts with Palm Sunday and ends on Easter Saturday.
I	Iconostasis	The screen, covered with icons, which separates the congregation from the altar in an Orthodox church.
	Icons	Special paintings of Jesus, the family of Jesus, the Virgin Mary or a saint; used as an aid to prayer in the Orthodox Church.
	Id-ul-Adha	The Muslim festival commemorating the willingness of the prophet Ibrahim (Abraham) to sacrifice his son, Isma'il (Ishmael), to God.
	Id-ul-Fitr	The Muslim festival marking the end of Ramadan.
	Imam	The man who leads the prayers and preaches the Friday sermon in a mosque.
	Infant baptism	The practice of baptising babies; followed by most Churches including the Roman Catholic, Orthodox and Anglican Churches.
	Israel	Also called Palestine; the modern country of Israel was formed in 1948.
J	Jerusalem	The city first captured by King David and the most sacred city to all Jews; it is also considered holy by Muslims and Christians.
	Jesus	The man whose life and teaching led to the foundation of the Christian Church; believed by Christians to be the Son of God.
K	Ka'bah	The cube-shaped shrine which stands in Makkah; visited by millions of pilgrims during the Hajj.
	Karma	'Action' or 'deed'; the Hindu belief that what a person does in this life leads to rewards or punishments in the next life.
	Kashrut	Food laws from the scriptures which govern the lives of Orthodox Jews.
	Khalsa	The Sikh religious brotherhood open to male and female believers; begun by the tenth Guru, Guru Gobind Singh, in 1699 CE.
	Kosher	'Fit' or 'proper'; used to describe food which is judged fit to eat under Jewish dietary laws.
	Krishna	One of the most popular Hindu gods; an avatar of Vishnu.
L	Langar	'Guru's kitchen'; the dining hall in a gurdwara and the food served there.
	Last Supper	The last meal that Jesus ate with his disciples before he was arrested and crucified.
	Lectern	The stand, often in the shape of an eagle, on which the Bible is placed in many churches.
	Lent	The season before Holy Week begins when Christians spend time in extra prayer and Bible study before the festival of Easter.
	Lord's Prayer	The prayer which, according to the Gospels, Jesus taught his followers to use; used in many churches as part of worship.
M	Madinah	The city that welcomed Muhammad and his followers in 622 CE after he left Makkah.
	Madrasah	The school where young Muslims are taught Arabic and the teachings of the Qur'an.
	Makkah	The birthplace of Muhammad in present-day Saudi Arabia.
	Mandalas	Symbolic drawings of the universe often made out of sand; particularly important in Tibetan Buddhism.
	Mandir	The Hindu place of worship.
	Mantra	A sacred formula or chant; used particularly in Hindu worship.
	Mass	The name given by Roman Catholics to the service of Holy Communion.
	Melas	Sikh festivals which are not gurpurbs.
	Messiah	The figure expected by Jews to lead them out of captivity; Christians believe that Jesus was the promised Messiah.

Middle Way	The way between a life of self-denial and a life of luxury taught by the Buddha as the heart of his teaching.
Mihrab	The niche in one wall of a mosque which indicates the direction of Makkah.
Monks	Men who devote themselves to a life of prayer and study; important in both Christianity and Buddhism.
Moses	The man who led the Jews out of Egyptian slavery; received the Ten Commandments and the Jewish Law from God on Mount Sinai.
Mosque	'Place of prostration'; the Muslim place of worship.
Muhammad	The last, and greatest, prophet in Islam; the one chosen by Allah to receive the revelations which are collected in the Qur'an.
Murtis	Hindu images or statues of God.

N

Nam	The Sikh name for God.
New Testament	The second part of the Christian Bible; it contains 27 books including the Gospels and the Epistles (letters) written by the early Christian leaders.
Nirvana	The final state of perfect peace which all Buddhists strive for.
Nonconformist Churches	Protestant Churches, such as the Baptist Church or Methodist Church, which separated from the Church of England in the seventeenth century.
Nuns	Women who give themselves to a life of prayer, study and service; particularly important in Christianity and Buddhism.

O

Old Testament	The Jewish scriptures included as the first part of the Christian Bible; contains 39 books.
Orthodox Church	Originally the Church of the Eastern region of the Roman Empire; separated from the Roman Catholic Church in 1054 CE.

P

Panj piares	'The five beloved ones'; those who were first initiated into Khalsa and the name used for those who perform the rite today.
Parables	Everyday stories told by Jesus which carry a spiritual or moral message.
Passover	The Jewish festival which commemorates the delivery of the Jews from slavery in Egypt.
Pentecost	The festival at which the followers of Jesus received the gift of the Holy Spirit.
Peter	The main disciple of Jesus; became the first leader of the Christian Church after Jesus had left the earth.
Prayer wheels	Cylinders used in Tibetan Buddhism and inscribed with Buddhist mantras; as the wheels turn they release the power of the mantra.
Priest	Someone ordained to the ministry in the Roman Catholic and Anglican Churches; given the authority to deliver the sacraments to the people.
Prophets	Men or women who pass on God's message to the people.
Pulpit	A raised platform in a church from where sermons are given.

Q

Qiblah	The direction which Muslims face when performing salah – towards Makkah.
Quakers	The Christian Church formed in the seventeenth century by George Fox; known for its largely silent form of worship and also known as the Society of Friends.
Qur'an	'That which is read or recited'; the divine book revealed to the Prophet Muhammad by Allah.

R

Rak'ah	A sequence of movements and prayers which make up part of the Muslim prayer routine.
Ramadan	The ninth month of the Islamic calendar; during this month all Muslims must fast from daybreak until sunset.
Reincarnation	The belief held by Hindus and Buddhists that the soul is reborn many times before being released.
Resurrection	The rising from the dead of Jesus on the third day after his crucifixion.

Roman Catholic Church	The oldest Christian Church; owes its allegiance to the Pope in Rome.
Rosary	A string of beads used by many Roman Catholics to help them with their thoughts and prayers.
Rosh Hashanah	The festival celebrating the Jewish New Year.
Rupas	'Forms'; images of the Buddha.

S

Sabbath Day	The seventh day of the week; a Jewish day of rest which lasts from Friday night to Saturday night.
Salah	The formal prayers undertaken by Muslims and recited in Arabic five times a day.
Salvation Army	The Protestant Church founded in the nineteenth century; known for its social work as well as its services.
Sanhedrin	The Jewish Council at the time of Jesus; Jesus appeared before its members when he was arrested.
Sewa	The Sikh obligation to serve others.
Stupas	Originally places where remnants of the ashes of the Buddha were buried; they have become places of pilgrimage for Buddhists.
Sukkoth	One of the three pilgrim festivals in the Jewish scriptures; a time when Jews from all over the Roman Empire travelled to Jerusalem to celebrate.
Sunday	The first day of the week; the Christian holy day since the fourth century.
Synagogue	The Jewish place of worship.

T

Takht	The throne on which the Guru Granth Sahib is placed in a gurdwara.
Tallit	The Jewish prayer shawl; a four-cornered garment with fringes.
Tefillin	Small leather boxes containing passages from the Torah, strapped on a Jewish man's arm and forehead for morning prayers on weekdays.
Temple	The Buddhist place of worship.
Ten Commandments	The ten laws which Jews believe were given to Moses by God on Mount Sinai; known by Jews as the Ten Sayings.
Torah	'Law' or 'teaching'; the first five books of the Jewish scriptures.
Turban	The head-covering expected to be worn by Sikh men.

V

Vicar	The priest in the Church of England who has responsibility for a church or churches.
Virgin Mary	Mary, the mother of Jesus; called the Virgin Mary by Roman Catholics who address prayers to her.

W

Wesak	A Buddhist festival that celebrates the birth, enlightenment and death of the Buddha.
Wudu	The ritual washing routine that Muslims follow before prayer.

Y

Yom Kippur	The Jewish Day of Atonement; the most solemn day of Jewish year which takes place ten days after Rosh Hashanah.